To Jerry.

With best wishes for
the future.

Chas. Pratley

23rd. Oct. 1977

The Folklore of The British Isles
General Editor : Venetia J. Newall

The Folklore of the Cotswolds

The Folklore of
the Cotswolds

Katharine M. Briggs

Drawings by Gay John Galsworthy

B. T. BATSFORD LTD LONDON

First published 1974
© Katharine M. Briggs 1974

0 7134 2831 7

Printed in Great Britain by
Bristol Typesetting Co. Ltd. Bristol
for the Publishers
B. T. Batsford Ltd 4 Fitzhardinge Street London W1H 0AH

Foreword

THE COTSWOLDS, running through the eastern part of Gloucestershire and overlapping into the nearby counties, lack administrative unity but are an area of marked economic, social and cultural identity. Uplands averaging 600 to 700 feet, their name indicates earlier afforestation, though sheep-rearing and quarrying brought the wealth which later shaped the district's character, with its wool-trading towns and stone buildings. The old forest survives only in Wychwood.

Wychwood Forest lies in the Oxfordshire Cotswolds, the corner of the county where Katharine Briggs herself lives. At Burford, her home for many years, she works in her lovely house, surrounded by an extensive folklore library. Her literary output, spread over forty years, has included poetry, plays and fiction, as well as her outstanding books on folklore. *A Dictionary of British Folk-Tales* (1970–1), a definitive work of reference comprising four large volumes, was the result of ten years solid research and has been internationally acclaimed. This was her seventh major work on folklore and now, in her 76th year, she has followed it with *The Last of the Astrologers* and the present volume.

I had the honour and pleasure of editing the *Festschrift* published on her 75th birthday (*The Witch Figure*; 1973) and the Appreciation contributed by Ruth Michaelis-Jena pointed to 'the world Katharine Briggs is concerned with, and to which she has introduced so many so successfully.' Writing of her myself, six years earlier, I referred to 'a lightness of touch unusual in eminent scholars.' Dr Briggs herself said, during a radio interview following publication of the *Festschrift*: 'Scholars didn't take folklore seriously because there has been a lot of very inferior writing on the subject', and, endorsing Peter Opie's view, she described folklore as 'the Cinderella of all the sciences.'

It is a historical coincidence that, over 200 years ago, Maria Edgeworth was born only a few miles from Burford. Percy Newby wrote of Miss Edgeworth's 'dignified and shrewd peasantry', and Katharine Briggs, whose own fictional works often draw on folkloric material, shows a similar unwavering respect for her subject matter. *Rackrent Castle* inspired the Waverley novels, and Scott mentions Maria Edgeworth in his 1814 postscript. These in turn, as Professor Dorson neatly puts it, 'sired books of tradition', and when folklore grew into a serious study later in the same century, 'books of tradition' became the norm. By contrast, Katharine Briggs, especially in her books on the 17th century, has applied her erudition and literary skill to demonstrating the breadth of our subject, and that folklore is not a fossil irrelevant to everyday life.

In fact, folklore is an element of our cultural unity, the social structure of which the folklorist himself forms part, and his own role within which he must fully understand if he is to function effectively. A nice story exists of Scott's informant, Mrs Murray Keith, when he disclaimed misuse of her stories: 'What, d'ye think that I dinna ken my ain groats among other folk's kail?' was her comment. But the folklorist must realise that the kail, too, is important. Oddly enough, urban lore, at one time held in some contempt, received early recognition when Scott's friend, Robert Chambers, published his *Traditions of Edinburgh* (1824). Considerable but spasmodic publication of available folklore material has occurred since, and in the 19th century, or even later, much of the collecting was done by local gentry, clergymen, doctors and the like. These categories have either dwindled in importance or, through changing times, possess neither the leisure nor the influence to make them privileged collectors. Yet, as Dr Briggs pointed out in her recent broadcast, their work is not negligible: they are 'people who are known and trusted and who will be told much more real things than somebody coming from outside.'

In this swift changing period, folklore, as a living force, develops at an accelerated pace. Its new aspects must be recorded and studied but, with scarcely over a century of serious collecting behind us, the rungs of cultural life provided by disappearing, or even remoulded, folk traditions risk being overlooked. *The Randwick Wap Modernised* (pages 183–6) differs from the Wap described by Hone, quoting an informant of 1827, not merely because minor details have changed. The whole psychological content has altered, just as the 1827 Wap varied in its essential psychology from those of earlier eras. Hence the description of a custom within any given context, in its various aspects, is as valuable as the factual details.

London University   Venetia Newall
June 1974.

Contents

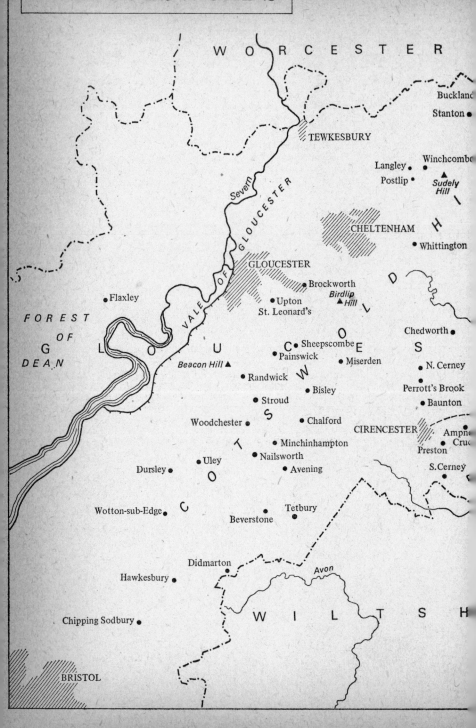

THE COTSWOLDS

W O R C E S T E R

Buckland
Stanton •

TEWKESBURY

Langley •   Winchcombe
Postlip •   *Sudely Hill*

CHELTENHAM

Severn

• Whittington

GLOUCESTER
• Brockworth
• Upton   *Birdlip Hill*
St. Leonard's

Chedworth •

• Flaxley

F O R E S T
O F
G   L
D E A N

Beacon Hill ▲

C • • Sheepscombe
Painswick   • Miserden

• N. Cerney

• Randwick

• Perrott's Brook
• Bisley   • Baunton

• Stroud

Woodchester •   • Chalford   CIRENCESTER   Ampne
                                                        Cruc
                                        Preston
• Minchinhampton   • S.Cerney

• Uley   • Nailsworth
Dursley •   • Avening

Wotton-sub-Edge •   • Tetbury
                Beverstone •

• Didmarton   *Avon*
Hawkesbury •

Chipping Sodbury •   W I L T S H

BRISTOL

Acknowledgements

For the reproduction of published material I have to thank the Rev Edward Rainsberry for permission to quote from *Through the Lych Gate* and the Cambridge Morris Men who kindly sent me a copy of their anniversary pamphlet with full permission to quote from it as I desired; and Miss Christina Hole, the editor of *Folklore*, for permission to quote from the publications of the Folklore Society and from the *Annual Record of the Oxfordshire and District Folk-Lore Society*.

The vicar of Painswick spared time on a very busy morning to give me a bunch of leaflets about the Painswick church and the Clipping Service.

I have also to thank many kind oral informants, Mrs Eileen Claridge of Charlbury, Mr Andrews of Swinbrook, Mr F. Abbott of Fulwell, Mrs Holloway of Shorthampton, Mr and Mrs E. Meadows of Snowshill, Mr George Powell of Stonesfield, Mr F. R. Watts of Stonesfield, Mrs J. Poore of Stonesfield, Mr and Mrs Pratley of Wilcote, Miss Ashby and Miss Phillips of Bledington, Mrs Rogers of Painswick, the Rev N. R. Morrison of Randwick Vicarage and the Rev Michael Bland of Buckland Rectory. Mrs Falconer, Mrs Groves and Mrs Haynes, to whom I owe much valuable information, have now died. I much regret the loss of further opportunities of talking to them. Mrs Renée Tickell, however, has kindly given me some further information, which I have included in Chapter 10, gleaned from her mother, Mrs Haynes, and I have to thank her for putting me in touch with Mrs Haynes in the first place.

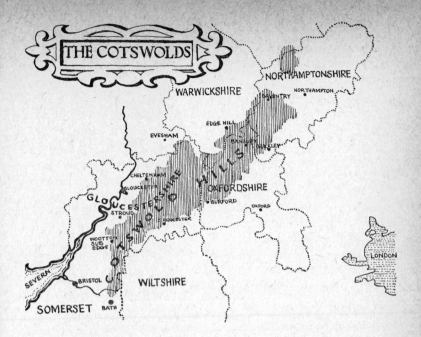

1 General Survey of the Cotswolds

THE COTSWOLDS ARE AN OUTCROP of that long spine of oolitic limestone that runs from Somerset up to Yorkshire, changing in colour and character from place to place. They cover a part of several counties: Oxfordshire, Gloucestershire, a little way into Warwickshire and an upthrust into Northamptonshire. The exact boundaries are not easy to fix, but they may be said to fade away very near to Burford on the south and to Edgehill on the north-west, to Daventry and Brackley on the north-east, jutting out further west to the escarpment which slopes sharply to the Gloucester Plain at Wootton-sub-Edge and to Worcestershire at Broadway. In Neolithic times roads and pathways avoided the swampy, wooded lowlands and followed the lines of the hills, therefore the Cotswolds show signs of very early habitation, with ancient track-ways running across and many menhirs, dolmens and barrows scattered about, with the famous circle of the Rollright Stones, more primitive in design than Stonehenge and with many legends clustering around it. These uplands were not however bare, like the chalky slopes of the Berkshire Downs, but covered in places by great forests. Wychwood was the eldest of these and the chief of them. It originally covered a great area and gave successive shelter to conquered peoples and tribes. It was so influential in the life and tradition of the Cotswolds that it deserves a chapter to itself. Round the outer borders of the forest are prehistoric earthworks and tombs which bear witness to its early habitation. There are round barrows near Asthall, Brize's Lodge, Chadlington, Ditchley, Enstone, Kiddington, Langley, Leafield, Sarsden, Shipton-under-Wychwood, Spelsbury, Swinbrook and Wootton. And this is only to cite a restricted area. In the same area there are square earthworks and the long Iron-Age fortification of Grim's Ditch, of which five lengths remain between Charlbury and Woodstock. On the western escarpment overhanging the Gloucester Plain and the Bristol Channel there is a long string of Neolithic and Iron-Age forts, mounds and burial chambers. Some of the more impressive are Hetty Pegler's Tump, near Uley, Nan Tow's Tump at Didmarton, the fine, multivallate hillfort at Sodbury and the Bulwarks at Minchinhampton. The traditions that have arisen about these remnants of long-past cultures are naturally of much later date than the artefacts for which they endeavour to account. Even the name ' Grimsditch' is unlikely to be earlier than Saxon times for ' Grim' was a name for Odin and this Iron-Age fortification probably pre-dated the Romans. Nan Tow's Tump at Didmarton is traditionally supposed to be the burial place of a witch, Nan Tow, who was buried standing upright inside it, and the Enstone Hoar Stone is said locally to mark the grave of an imaginary General Hoar, killed in the Civil War. ' Hoar Stone' is however a common name for a standing stone in the Cotswold area. Some archaeologists suppose the word to be ' War Stone', a plausible conjecture, since the initial ' w' and the initial ' h' are both omitted in the Cotswold dialect. It is spoken of as an ' oar stone'. Evidence given by Mr Abbott, a septuagenarian of Fulwell, near Enstone, on 27 April 1973 made no claim for so late a date as the Civil War. He merely called it ' A long time ago; I couldn't say how long.' He recorded an interesting tradition that the body was brought along Dead Man's Ride by a man, a horse and a dog. Dead Man's Ride is an indistinctly marked track which may have originally been part of Grim's Ditch, a short length of which appears in a line with the track west of Ditchley. A ghost tradition is attached to this and Mr Abbott himself claimed to have seen two men going along Dead Man's Ride and passing straight through the wire-netting fence. His dogs crouched and bristled and would not move till the ghosts had passed. It may be remarked that Mr Abbott, pointing out a large slab of stone lying undressed in the disused quarry, called it 'an oar stone', so that possibly the word only means a large, undressed stone.

The Tingle Stone at the long barrow near Avening is one of the moving stones, like the Somerset Wimble Stone. It is said to run round the field when it hears the church clock strike midnight. This of course can be taken in two ways.

The fullest traditional stories are appropriately told about the most impressive of the Cotswold monuments, the Rollright Stones. These consist of an upshaped circle, of roughly the same diameter as Stonehenge with a tall dolmen on the other side of the ancient trackway about 50 yards to the west, called the King-Stone, and the remains of a long barrow, called the Whispering Knights, about a quarter of a mile to the east. Faint traces of many sepulchral monuments are found in the district, so that the whole area seems to have been a kind of rough Stonehenge. The Rollright Stones were described by Camden in the sixteenth century, by Robert Plot in the seventeenth and by Sheldon and Stukeley in the eighteenth but the fullest account of the traditions surrounding them is given by A. J. Evans in *The Folklore Journal* of 1895. According to the legend the king was at the head of an invading army. He had heard a prophecy that if he could see Long Compton he would be king of all England. Long Compton lay in the Warwickshire valley just below him. He left his army encamped and a group of malcontent knights whispering traitorously at a little distance and strode up the slope to the top of the ride. He had almost reached it when he met a witch, presumably from Long Compton, which was famous for them till almost the present day. She chanted out to him:

> Seven long strides thou shalt take,
> And if Long Compton thou can see,
> King of England thou shalt be.

The king lengthened his stride, shouting exultantly:

> Stick, stock, stone!
> As King of England I shall be known!

As he took the seventh stride a long barrow of earth rose up in
front of him and the witch sang out:

> As Long Compton thou canst not see
> King of England thou shalt not be.
> Rise up stick, and stand still, stone
> For King of England thou shalt be none;
> Thou and thy men *hoar* stones shall be
> And I myself an eldern tree.

All were at once transformed, but the transformation was not
complete. One day they say the spell will be broken and the king
and his army will set out afresh to conquer England. In the meantime the Whispering Knights go down the hill at midnight to drink
from the spring in Little Rollright spinney. Opinions differ as to
whether they go down every night or only on certain holy days. At
midnight too, it is said that the stones of the circle come to life for
a moment and dance round in the air. The king is also said, like
the Tingle Stone, to go down to drink the water 'when he hears
the church clock strike midnight'. As for the elder witch, she has
been variously located, as one tree dies and another grows up. It is
also said that at midsummer when she is in flower she will bleed
if she is cut. On Midsummer Eve people formed a ring round the
King-Stone while one man cut the eldern witch. As she bled the
King-Stone moved his head. All elders are supposed to be witches
or fairy trees and to bleed if they are cut.

The dancing festivities with cakes and ale described by Stukeley
were probably held on Midsummer Eve. Girls used to go one by one
up to the Knights to listen to them whispering in hopes of divining
their own fate. The fairies were said to dance round the King Stone,
coming out of a hole near. An old man, Will Hughes, who was
recently dead when Evans wrote, claimed to have seen them and
his widow, Betsy Hughes, knew the hole and used as a child to put
a stone over it to keep the fairies underground. Chips from the King
Stone were considered lucky and travellers liked to carry them but
it was thought dangerous to move the stones; anyone who did so
was forced by the consequent ill-luck to restore them. A later
tradition was that it was impossible to count the stones. A baker who

had 75 loaves in his cart determined to count them by putting a loaf on each stone but when he had gone round the ring he found that the first loaves had vanished, so he leapt into his cart and drove away at top speed, determined not to try again. A vague tradition of sanctity hung about the place in old days. These various fragments of belief and primitive custom show how long a feeling of numinousness hangs about pagan sacred places.

After the Celts had pushed Neolithic men into the forests, the Romans came in their turn, drove great roads over the primitive trackways and designed a new network of communications on the lower lands. They made Cirencester their great centre in the Cotswold area and scattered pleasant villas about the countryside – Chedworth, North Leigh and Woodchester and many others. The Celtic and Roman pantheon mingled, as we can tell from the statues to the *Matronae* and from many well legends. It seems likely that some of our modern fairies, as, for instance, the brownies, may have sprung from this hybrid. It is interesting to notice how many of the mosaic pavements that remain to us represent Orpheus charming the beasts. One of our Middle-English romances is *King Orfeo*, a fairy-story version of Orpheus and Eurydice. The legend was evidently popular in Romano-Celtic Britain and retained its popularity beyond the Saxon era into the Norman. It is said however that the mosaic workers of Cirencester specialised so much in the Orpheus tradition that their work may be recognised by the introduction of this theme. The late Roman Empire was made up of a fantastic mixture of nationalities and it is hard to guess what was left when the Roman legions were drawn back to the metropolis, but from the Celtic traditions that persisted in Saxon England it is clear that the Celtic element was still strong.

The Saxons came, and after them the Norsemen; both left their heritage of historic legends and outlaw tales and such saints' legends as that of St Kenelm, but, though there are Norse spirits in the north-west and the east of England, in the Cotswolds the Celtic traditions seem on the whole to be the strongest and most persistent.

After the Norman Conquest the pattern that emerges is that of the royal hunting forests with their lodges and outlaws, the feudal tenure and strip cultivation, the sheep walks and the stone quarries. For the forests, the memory of the hunting monarchs is still fresh in tradition, with tales of outlaws, robbers and deer-stealers. The forests gradually shrank from the thirteenth century onwards and sheep walks and farms took the place of the open fields.

From the twelfth century sheep and wool were an important part of the Cotswold economy, though in the early days the sheep were so small that a whole fleece weighed no more than 2lbs. Even the villein made something on the sale of his wool and by the fourteenth century wool had become the great export of England and Cotswold wool was the best of all. The Lord Chancellor's Woolsack is a memorial to that staple industry and for a year or so more we still retain the 14-lb stone which reminds us of the traditional method of computing a fleece.

By the fourteenth century the best and heaviest of fleeces weighed 28lbs each. The merchant, riding round to buy his wool, would carry three weights strapped to his saddle: one of 7lbs, one of 4 and one of 3. The farmer awaiting him would have a simple set of scales like a seesaw, with a stone whittled down to weigh 14lbs in one scale. The merchant's three tested weights would be set against it and then the four weights were put together on one side and the fleeces one by one on the other. Wool would have to be added till the scales hung even, the farmer and the merchant would each mark his tally and in this manner the weighing and paying would be done without need for long accounts and then packed by the merchant's man for despatch. This then is how a stone came to be reckoned as 14lbs.

Another common trace of the wool trades is the presence of the wool-staplers' tombs in so many of the Cotswold churchyards. These are rounded altar-tombs, ridged to represent corded bales of wool and were supposed to be used only for those merchants who had the right to ship their wools from the 14 wool-staple towns which regulated the export wool trade. In the fourteenth century Bristol was added to these as the Cotswold wool trade became more considerable. Actually these tombs were often used for lesser men, for Burford churchyard contains several fine examples, though Burford was devoted to subsidiary wool trades and had no staple merchants.

Cotswold wool and Cotswold stone are linked together in most people's minds because of the great wool churches of the fourteenth century. Cotswold stone was used far beyond the Cotswolds and for a long period of time. Once Taynton quarries were among the most famous and the oldest and were worked in Roman times. A Roman stone coffin, 7ft 7ins in length, which was found on the south bank of the Windrush in 1814, was made of Taynton stone. The Taynton quarries were very extensive, with near-by workings at Barrington, Burford, Upton, Windrush and Milton, though none yielded such a high quality of stone as the Taynton quarries. These yielded the four different types of stone to be found in the Cotswolds; the forest marble, used for interior decoration, fireplaces and the like; the high-quality freestone, suitable for shaping and carving; the ironstone, used for troughs because it withstood heat and cold, and the white limestone suitable only for rough walling and road-making.

There was one type of stone not to be found in any quantity in Taynton quarries and that was the Stonesfield roofing slate found between Charlbury and Woodstock. This was a stone laid down in remarkably even layers which split very readily in frost when first it was exposed to the air. All the oolitic limestones develop a hard crust after weathering and they were normally cut into the size required for building and stacked up to weather. The Stonesfield slates on the other hand were cut out in large blocks and covered with earth until the first frosts came. When this happened, generally in the middle of a wintry night, the church bell was rung, everyone tumbled out of bed, swept off the earth and poured water over the slabs of slate. Then they could go peacefully back to bed and wait for the frost to work for them. As one can see from this, the quarrymen generally lived in a close community. They were independent, intelligent men, tough and enterprising, often keen poachers, with many songs and traditions in common. Not many of the quarries are now working, though Mr Lea of Taynton has reopened his ancient and famous quarry and now works it single-handed. Mr George Swinford, who got together and owns Filkins Folk Museum, is one of the last of the quarrymen and has many traditions to tell. He explored the great mined quarries at Barrington before they were filled in. The workings went directly under the New Inn on the London–Cheltenham Road. The landlady provided hot meals for the quarrymen and when the dinner was ready she used to bang on the kitchen floor to call them up. This strikes a homely note, but the stones from these quarries went far afield. In the seventeenth century Christopher Kempster, Wren's favourite mason, shipped stone at Radcot Bridge and sent it down the Thames to help in the rebuilding of St Paul's. He built Tom Tower at Oxford too and from the thirteenth to the nineteenth century Oxford was enriched with stone from these upland quarries.

B

2 Seasonal Customs and Festivities

THE WHEELING YEAR went round in the Cotswolds as in other parts of England, spangled with festivals which sprang from the marriage of the Christian Church with prehistoric practices and beliefs. There were regional and local variations, though these were sometimes more apparent than real. History accounted for some of the differences: where the Puritans were strong, ancient usages, correctly thought to be pagan, were repressed and in time died out. Sometimes however the absence of any mention of a custom comes from the absence of an observing eye and a recording pen.

It is difficult to know which spoke of the year to start with, for the New Year is only half-way through the 12 days of Christmas. It would seem appropriate to start with Plough Monday, which old Gervase Markham in his *English Husbandman* chose as the beginning of the farming year. 'The beginning of the year with husbandmen is at Plow Day, being ever the first Munday after

Twelfth-day, at which time you shall goe forth with your draught and begin to plow.' This was a day marked with ceremonies in many counties but I have found no mention of them in the Cotswolds, perhaps because of the cold on the uplands, which gave rise to the proverb 'as late as Cotswold bere' (barley). Perhaps it is best to start on 2 February with Candlemas Day, the Feast of the Purification of the Virgin, when in most places the Christmas greens must be taken down and box and bay set up. This is not invariable; sometimes they were taken down on Epiphany and in later times even on Boxing Day. Candlemas Day was the time when candles were lighted to strengthen the power of the sun but paradoxically it was also the time when lights were extinguished. In an article in the *Annual Record of the Oxfordshire and District Folklore Society* for 1950 we are told: 'On Candlemas Day we always used to have tea without a light, as the days were supposed to have lengthened sufficiently by then to make this possible.' An old rhyme said:

> Candlemas Day, put beans in the clay:
> Put candles and candlesticks all away.

Bad weather was considered a good omen on Candlemas Day:

> If Candlemas is fair and clear,
> There'll be two winters in the year

is the gist of many sayings. In Minchinhampton, however, a contrary saying is recorded. Miss J. Partridge was told by her charwoman in 1916: 'If it rains on Candlemas it will rain for about forty days after.' Snowdrops were generally feared as ominous of death but an exception was made for them on Candlemas Day, when they were supposed first to flower, for they were sacred to the Virgin. Before the Reformation candles were blessed and handed out on Candlemas Day and pious people lighted them to say their prayers by.

The next day of special importance to the young was St Valentine's Day, 14 February. The article on calendar customs which I have already quoted says, 'On St Valentine's Day young people sent Valentines to their sweethearts. There was a saying that if a dark man crossed the threshold on February 14th, a single daughter of the house would marry him before the year was out.'

It was often believed that the first man met by a maiden on St Valentine's Day would be her husband. This was from the fifteenth century believed to be also the mating day of the birds. Valentine cards were sent before Christmas cards though presents were given on St Valentine's Day before cards came into use. A pair of gloves was thought specially suitable. In the seventeenth century the choosing of a Valentine for the year was often sportive and was not in any way tantamount to an engagement. The Valentines for the year were often drawn by lot as a kind of game.

Not all festival days could be affixed to a regular annual date, for there were movable feasts as well as fixed ones. The chief of these was Easter which determined the dates of the days dependent on it, both before and after. Other movable festivals were those that fell on a day of the week, like Plough Monday – the Monday after Twelfth Night – in which there would necessarily be a slight variation. Certain saints' days were important in places whose churches were dedicated to them. So it will be seen that the Snowshill mummers' play, normally performed at Christmas, was played at Snowshill on St Barnabas Day:

> St Barnaby Bright;
> The longest Day and the shortest Night.

Shrove Tuesday was the first day tied up with the date of Easter. It was the day on which people confessed their sins and were shriven before the austerities of Lent and it combined the penitential and the carnival aspects of the season. The day before was often called 'Collop Monday' because the last meat of the season was eaten. This took the form of roast collops of bacon or of mutton. Eggs were going to be of prime importance in the next six weeks and poultry had an important place in the Shrove Tuesday rites. Hens who had not laid satisfactorily were whipped and it was the great season for cockfighting and cockshying. Shrove Tuesday was also Pancake Day. The Shroving Bell, which rang to call people to confession, was later called 'the Pancake Bell'. When it rang, housewives ran to their doors with their pans in their hands and tossed their pancakes. In some places they had, and still have, pancake races but these were less common in the Cotswolds. In some places too, hard-boiled eggs were a feature of Shrovetide as well as of Easter. This might suggest an earlier and more austere fast, as in the Orthodox Church, in which eggs were regarded as meat. The simplest way of preserving eggs is to boil them hard, and Shrove Tuesday pancakes would be the last chance of enjoying fresh eggs for some time. Eggs would be set under hens and hatch out Easter chickens, and those left over would be hard-boiled.

The next landmark in the Lenten season was Mothering Sunday in mid-Lent. This, like Shrovetide, was originally an ecclesiastical practice. It was the day on which the mother church or the cathedral was visited by the outlying churches and the custom was extended to human relationships and became one of the gentlest and most humane of the seasonal festivities. The calendar customs article already cited speaks of it briefly:

A pleasant Custom was observed on Mothering Sunday. Boys and girls whose work took them away from home returned to visit their Mothers, bringing with them a fruit cake and a bunch of primroses and violets which they had picked in the fields and hedgerows.

The cakes were generally baked by the mistresses and were often rich simnel cakes with almond paste mixed loosely through them. The most generally accepted derivation of the name is from the Latin *simila*, which means the finest flour, but tradition has supplied a jocular derivation in the story of a man and his wife, Sim and Nell, who quarrelled about how the cake should be cooked; one wanted it boiled and the other baked, so finally they compounded their differences and did both.

At Wotton-under-Edge and particularly at the Swan Inn, Mothering Sunday took rather a different form, for the servants there were allowed to invite their family and friends and were served with cakes and wine. Frumenty was another dish eaten on Mothering Sunday, which is also called Refreshment Sunday because the Lenten fast was broken on that day. This custom has been to a certain extent revived in many churches. At morning service the children come up to the altar rails where bunches of flowers are distributed among them. They then present the flowers to their mothers.

In England in earlier times pussy-willow catkins were called palms, and they were brought on Palm Sunday into the church to be blessed and taken home to bring blessing and good fortune to the houses. Palm Sunday was Fig Pudding Day. Passion Sunday was called 'Carl Sunday' or 'Carlin Sunday' and peas and beans were made into puddings and eaten on those days. 'Carline' was a name for pulse, so there may have been a kind of pun in the word; but it must be remembered that beans were supposed to be the food of the dead.

Good Friday was a day of mourning and many activities were

fatal on that day. No housewife would ever wash clothes on Good Friday. It was however a suitable day for sowing parsley, which was a very tricky plant. However, Good Friday after service time suited it best.

Bread and water was the monastic fare on Good Friday but there was one festive article of diet in most houses, the hot-cross buns which were sold in the streets and eaten at breakfast. Any uneaten were kept and dried and, finely powdered, were considered curative for all kinds of disorders.

Easter is the central festival of the Christian year and everywhere it is celebrated as a time of renewal. In the Cotswolds as elsewhere country people used to believe that the sun danced on Easter morning. It gave three springs in the air just as it rose and many were ready to swear that they actually saw it doing so. On Easter Sunday all who could do so came out in a new outfit and those who could not afford a complete outfit must at least have one new garment to show, or the birds would make droppings on them. An Easter bonnet was the favourite. A fine Easter was a prognostic of good weather:

> Rain Easter Day,
> Plenty of grass but little good hay

was a local saying. Coloured eggs were given at Easter but there seems no record of Easter egg-rolling, tempting though the close-cropped slopes must have been. Roast lamb, where it was obtainable, was the Easter dish, with tansy pudding, perhaps in commemoration of the Passover feast with its bitter herbs. The rule against eating meat was already relaxed on Holy Saturday and the dish on that day was bacon and eggs. If red herrings were still eaten they were cut to represent a horseman riding away. On Holy Saturday and Easter Monday in Aubrey's time Oxfordshire boys went round begging for meat and singing the song beginning:

> Herrings, Herrings, white and red
> Two a penny, Lent's dead.

If they were refused they were likely to play unpleasant tricks on the householders.

Easter Monday was the day for hunting the hare, for football and other sports and for stobball at Wotton-under-Edge and in that area.

At Minchinhampton a gigantic game of thread-the-needle used to be played on Easter Monday and on Easter Monday the Leafield people maintained, and still believe, that they have the right to go into Wychwood Forest and make 'Spanish water', which is made from a stick of liquorice put into a bottle filled up with water from one of the sacred springs in Wychwood Forest. The bottle is then shaken till the liquorice is dissolved. This is believed to be not only a tonic but a sovereign remedy for all kinds of disorders. It is a grievance to the Leafield people that Wychwood is now closed to them.

The second Sunday after Easter is Hocktide when there is a kind of war between men and women. It was observed more in the North of England than the Midlands but at Dursley in Gloucester two Hock days were observed from the sixteenth to the eighteenth century. On Hock Monday the men put ropes across the streets and taxed all passers-by and on Hock Tuesday the women did the same. Robert Plot records the same custom for Oxfordshire but he puts the women's day on the Monday and the men's on the Tuesday and says the women's is a more solemn rite and the men's inconsiderable.

Randwick and some of the neighbouring places had different customs. Hock Sunday was called Balaam's Ass Day because of the Old Testament lesson read on that day. There was possibly a miracle play performed there in earlier times, and people had got into the habit of coming. Whatever the origin of the custom, much was made of the reading and the church and even the church-yard used to be crowded. The same was true of Hawkesbury near Chipping Sodbury. On the next day, Hock Monday, 'Runnick Swop' – or 'Wap' as it is now called – was held and the Mock Mayor was elected with great merriment. The mayor was chaired through the town and set down in a shallow pond near the church while the Runnick Weavers' Song was sung. The eighteenth cen-tury *Gentleman's Magazine* version of this runs as follows:

> When Archelus began to spin
> And Pollo wrought upon a loom,
> Our trade to flourish did begin,
> Tho' conscience went to selling broom . . .

In the modern version 'Archelus' is interpreted as 'Hercules', but it was clear that Achilles was meant, whose mother concealed him among her maidens and set him to spin so as to avoid the death that was fated for him.

At the end of the song the mayor suddenly splashed all his attendants with water and the whole company moved off to the Rising Sun Inn, where they sang and drank till 11.30 p.m. In old times festivity and riot was kept up for several days. Later the ceremony was moved to May Day to coincide with the Randwick Cheese Rolling which was held on that date. It has now been shifted again to the first Saturday after May Day but it is still carried on with great animation, and the Runnick Wap is a notable occasion. At Randwick three double Gloucester cheeses are blessed and rolled round the churchyard. The Brockworth Cheese-Rolling took place on the slopes of Cooper's Hill on Whit Monday. It was moved this year to the Spring Holiday Monday.

Bisley church was heavily restored in the nineteenth century but it has been a sacred site since pre-Christian days and several Roman pagan altars were discovered during its restoration. Seven springs flow out close together at the base of the steep mound on which the church is built and it is said that sacred rites were performed at them. The Bisley well-dressing, however, which fills the church to overflowing every Ascension-tide, was devised and instituted in 1863 by Thomas Keble, John Keble's younger brother. It is a flower ceremony but not so elaborate as the Derbyshire well-dressing. The seven springs flow out of the hill into built-up pools with high walls behind them. After a service the children of the village go in procession down to the wells, the foremost ones carrying floral initials which are hung up above the wells to form the word ' Ascension' and the date. This ceremony has now been carried on with unabated enthusiasm for over a hundred years.

We must now go back from the festivals dated by Easter to the fixed festivals which we have passed over.

The first of March, St David's Day, is marked by no special festivities in the Cotswolds, though there, as elsewhere, it is believed that it is the day on which fleas, called ' the black army' get into the house. ' I don't want the black soldiers in,' as an old villager in Minchinhampton, who was most careful to keep every window shut on 1 March lest fleas should enter, said.

Many churches flew St George's flag on St George's Day. The St Mark's vigil, so popular in the North and the East seems to have got no nearer the Cotswolds than Northamptonshire. One hears little even of April Fool's Day. The first great day of the spring was May Day. Formerly the night in the woods bringing in the May was devoted to fertility rites. It was never christianised and was understandably more hated by the Puritans than any other festival. This was the special time of the Morris dancers, the setting up of the Maypole and summer halls and bowers, of the Robin Hood plays, the treading of the mazes, cakes and ale and kisses. Stubbes' denunciation of the May games in the sixteenth century conveys a zest and gusto which is quite unforgettable. By the middle of the nineteenth century the May games had not been forgotten but they had been taken over by children. A few true Maypoles were still set up, particularly where the Morris dancers survived. Bledington had one till 1924 and Chipping Campden's has survived to this day. On the whole, however, May Day tended to belong to the schoolchildren. The well-known Gloucestershire Maypole Song reads as if it had been made up by a village school-mistress:

> Round the Maypole trit-trit-trot
> See what a Maypole we have got!
> Fine and gay,
> Trip away,
> Happy is our new May-day.

The description of the children's May Day at the end of the nineteenth century given by Flora Thompson in *Lark Rise* can hardly be bettered. Some shape and tradition was still left to it and it was a matter of deep emotion to the children and not without significance to the older people who had delegated their performance to the young ones. It seems to have been the courting generation who were missed out. The May garland and the 'lady' were still of deep significance to the children and are most carefully described:

The foundation of the garland was a light wooden framework of uprights supporting graduated hoops, forming a bell-shaped structure almost four feet high. This frame was covered with flowers, bunched and set closely, after the manner of wreath-making.

The covering of this garland was a day's work, and 30 April was devoted to it in the schools. Some of the boys had walked six or eight miles on the Sunday before to fetch primroses from distant woods and a great store of flowers, wild and cultivated was needed to cover the frame. The final top knot was made of crown imperials

and the mound was sprinkled and left for the night. In the meantime the queen's crown was made of garden daisies, for daisies were
flowers of magic significance. White and red ones were used on a
background of evergreens. In the morning the ' lady ' was added to
the garland, a large china doll in a blue dress arranged to sit on
a little ledge in the centre front of the garland. Great reverence was
paid to the lady. The whole structure was covered with a veil and
the procession set out. The officials consisted of a boy with a flag,
a girl with a money-box, the garland with two bearers, the king
and queen, two maids of honour, a lord and lady, two more maids
of honour, a footman and a footman's lady, the rank and file, walking in twos, a girl known as mother and a boy called ragman. The
mother carried a market basket with the lunch of the performers,
the boy everyone's coats in case of rain. Both boys and girls were
decked out with ribbons and the girls wore white or light-coloured
frocks and veils. All who could get them wore white gloves, though
these were not often obtainable. It is clear that this elaborate
organisation was inherited from an adult ritual. The song, too, was
one of the true May-Day songs, ' A bunch of may I have brought
you . . .'. This song was, however, despised by the children as old-
fashioned and something more special was practised in response to
a munificent donation: ' All hail, gentle Spring', or ' Come see
our new garland, so green and so gay'.

There were adult May-Day celebrations at Lower Heyford, North
Leigh, Spelsbury, Chipping Campden, Bledington, Randwick, and
Nailsworth but, perhaps because of the lateness of the Cotswold
spring, many ceremonials suitable to May were performed at Whit-
suntide. The most famous of all the Whitsuntide events were
Dover's Cotswold Games, which took place on Whit Thursday on
Dover's Hill in the parish of Weston-sub-Edge and a mile from
Chipping Campden. Captain Dover, as he was called because he
was captain of the games, was an attorney, born in 1575 at Barton-
on-the-Heath in Warwickshire. Anthony Wood in his *Athenae
Oxoniensis* gives an account of the games and of the collection of
poems, *Annalia Dubrensia* which were written to celebrate it:

This book which hath the running title on every page, of Cotswold Games, consists of verses made by several hands on the said
Annalia Dubrensia, but nothing of the Cotswold Muse of Barks-
dale refers to them, which some, who have only seen the title of
it, think to be the same. The said games were begun, and con-

tinued at a certain time in the year for forty years, by one Rob. Dover – who being full of activity, and of a generous, free and public spirit, did with leave from King James I, select a place on Cotswold Hills in Gloucestershire, whereon those games should be acted. Endimion Porter, Esq., a native of that county, and a servant to that king, a person of a most generous spirit, did, to encourage Dover give him some of the king's old cloaths, with a hat and feather and ruff, purposely to grace him and consequently the solemnity. Dover was constantly in person well mounted and accoutred, and was the chief director and manager of those games frequented by the nobility and gentry (some of whom came 60 miles to see them) even till the rascally rebellion was begun by the Presbyterians, who gave a stop to their proceedings, and spoiled all that was generous or ingenious elsewhere. The verses in the said book called ' Annalia Dubrensia ', were composed by several poets, some of which were then the chiefest of the nation, as Michael Drayton; Thomas Randolph of Cambridge; Ben. Johnson; Owen Feltham; Capt. John Menese; Shakerley Marmyon; Thomas Heywood; etc. Before the said book of ' Annalia Dubrensia ' is a cut representing the games and sports, as men playing at cudgels, wrestling, leaping, pitching the bar, throwing the iron hammer, handling the pyke, leaping over the heads of men kneeling, standing upon their hands, etc. Also the dancing of women, men hunting and coursing the hare with hounds and greyhounds, etc., with a castle built of boards on a hillock with guns therein.

The book was reproduced with an introduction and notes by E. R. Vyvyan in 1970 and is very well worth study. Among the sports shown in the frontispiece and not mentioned by Wood is the game of shin-kicking – described by George Swinford in the next chapter – leap-frog, small-sword play with wooden, basket-hilted swords, a pleasant, formal picnic and what appears to represent an elaborate maze.

As Wood said, the Civil War ended the Cotswold Games for a time, but they were revived soon after the Restoration, and continued to be played with diminishing respectability until 1851 when they had become so great a nuisance in the neighbourhood that they were stopped by Act of Parliament.

The other most popular event was the Whit Hunt in Wychwood Forest, in which the villages round Witney all took part.

Manning gives an account of it in Volume VIII of *Folklore*, drawn
from Ackerman's *Ancient Limits of Wychwood Forest*. The head-
quarters of the hunt was Ducklington, just outside the limits of the
Cotswolds. The villagers were all roused at midnight on Whit
Sunday by the blowing of 'peeling horns', made of green willow
bark, peeled in a spiral strip after long soaking. At daybreak on
Monday they rode off to Hailey on the edge of the forest, where
they were joined by a crowd of hunters from Witney, Bampton,
Brize Norton, Crawley, Leafield, Charlbury, Finstock and other
hamlets. They killed three deer, one claimed by Hailey, one by
Crawley and one by Witney. The man who was first in at the death
of the deer claimed the head and antlers. The skin was cut up and
distributed. In the meantime the Maypole was put up in Ducklington and the 'bowery', a big barn, was dressed up and decorated with
flowers. When the hunters returned a feast called the 'Youth Ale'
was held in the bowery. All the week the Morris dancers went out
to the neighbouring villages and returned to revel in the bowery.
On Saturday the deer was cooked and eaten. These practices went
on till 1847. At the other side of the forest there was a similar
Whitsun hunt right claimed by the townspeople of Burford. But,
just as foot and mouth disease has closed many rights of way in the
present century, so the incidence of plague was the occasion for
breaking off the hunting in 1593 and soon the right was commuted
for the gift of two bucks and a fawn to be delivered at Capp's
Lodge to the Lord and Lady of Whitsun, a boy and girl chosen from
the town. These deer were hunted in the fields and a feast of venison
held by all the town. This ceremony went on till 1827 and the deer
were sent down till 1854, when £150 was given to the corporation
in lieu of the annual gift. This went into the town charities. By this
time the forest had shrunken considerably.

Burford had other Whitsuntide celebrations, the most notable of
which was a procession in which the Burford dragon and giant were
borne down the hill. Camden the antiquary records this in his
Britannia and says that the dragon was carried down in memory of
a battle between the Saxons and Mercians in the eighth century, in
which the Saxons were victorious. Why the giant joined in the
procession Camden did not know but the processions were held both
at Whitsun and on John the Baptist's Day, the patronal festival of
the town.

Cirencester was another place where Whitsuntide was given great
prominence, with a lord and lady, musicians, dancers and a mace

bearer. The procession was formerly shallowly carved on the north wall of the church but it was plastered over in one of the nineteenth-century restorations. I have already mentioned Brockworth for its cheese-rolling, which started at a Maypole set up on top of the hill.

Mummers' plays generally belonged to Christmas but they were considered appropriate for any festival time and at Snowshill they were performed on 11 June, St Barnabas' Day, which was the patronal festival of the church. Few of the earlier inhabitants of Snowshill are left and the play has fallen into disuse but Mr Meadows, who took the part of Father Christmas, has kindly given me a copy of the text. It is a good representative play, with Jack Finney as the Doctor's attendant, and it is worth transcribing it.

Characters

Father Christmas	
King George	⎫
Bold Slasher	⎬ Dressed as soldiers
Doctor	Dressed in top hat and long-tailed coat
John Vinney	Dressed as a groom
Beelzebub	Dressed in tattered coat and long beard : looks rough : carries club and frying pan
Fiddler Wit	Like a man in the street with a fiddle : black face : some thin strips of rag on his coat

All have their faces painted.

———————

Father Christmas knocks at the door, is let in carrying a broom. He begins sweeping the room and says:
  In comes I, old Father Christmas, Christmas or not,
  I hope old Father Christmas will never be forgot;
  Roast beef, plum pudding and mince pies.
  Never did old Father Christmas like these better than I.
  A room, a room, a gallant room and give us room to reign,
  For we to show our bold activities this merry Christmas time.
  King George, and clear the way!
                    (Sweeps floor.)

King George:
>   In comes I, King George, King George, this noble knight,
>   Who shed his blood for Britons bright;
>   What makes me carry this blood weapon
>   Is because I have fought many a hard battle at home and
>   abroad;
>
>   And if any man here can conquer me
>   A French Captain Collier he shall be.

Father Christmas:
>   Walk in, Bold Slasher.

Bold Slasher:
>   Bold Slasher, Bold Slasher, Bold
>   Slasher is my name;
>   I come to fight this champion,
>   King George is called his name;
>   I'll cut him, I'll hack him,
>   I'll cut him as small as flies
>   And send him to Jamaica
>   To make mince pies.

King George:
>   Mince pies I do not like but a battle with you I will fight.
>   (They go to battle and King George is slain.)

Father Christmas:
>   Oh, is there a doctor to be found all ready near at hand?
>   Who'll cure this deep and deadly wound and make this
>   dead man stand?

Doctor (walks in):
>   Oh, yes, there is a doctor to be found all ready at hand,
>   Who will cure that deep and deadly wound and make that
>   dead man stand.

Father Christmas:
>   What canst thee cure?

Doctor:
Oh, I can cure imples, pimples, simples, itch, the
Stitch, the palsy and the gout;
Pain within and pains without;
And if the old man is in him I can fetch him out.

Father Christmas:
What is thy fee then, Doctor?

Doctor:
Five pounds my fee;
Ten pounds I ask before I set that gallant free.

Father Christmas:
Work thy will then, Doctor.

Doctor:
Where does this very bad pain lie?

Father Christmas:
In his upper lower jaw.

Doctor:
How long has he suffered this very bad pain?

Father Christmas:
A fortnight or three weeks before it came.

Doctor:
Why did you not send to me before it came?

Father Christmas:
'Cos I didn't know where thee lived.

Doctor:
I lives here and nowhere else long;
I bin up in the Black Country 'mongst the Gentiles,
        killing all and curing none;
Italy, Sicily, France and Spain, now I return to
        old England again.
                (Calls his assistant, John Vinney.)

Jack Vinney!

J. Vinney:
My name is not Jack Vinney.
Doctor:
What is thy name?

J. Vinney:
My name is Mr John Vinney, a man of great strength.
Do as much as thee or any other man;
Chop a good magpie's yud off and throw him in the ditch
And fetch him out in three months' time
As good a magpie as ever you did see.
Walk up and down the street in a purr of pattens.

Doctor:
That's all very fine, John, what other diseases?

J. Vinney:
Just as your medicine pleases.

Doctor:
Fetch me my spectacles, Jack Vinney.

J. Vinney:
Shan't; fetch 'em theeself then.

Doctor:
What's that?
(J. Vinney goes running to fetch them out of his haversack.)

J. Vinney:
Just a'coming, sir.
(Doctor puts on spectacles and examines the man.)

Doctor:
Ah, ah, ladies and gentlemen; this man is suffering from
the toothache very bad indeed. Fetch my pliers, Jack Vinney.

J. Vinney:
Fetch 'em theeself, then.

Doctor:
   What's that?

J. Vinney:
   Just a'coming, sir.
            (Runs to get them out of the haversack.)

Doctor:
   Now, my men, as strong as elephants,
   See if you can ease this poor man for me.

(Doctor on bended knees, with pliers and a horse's tooth hidden
in his hands; J. Vinney and Bold Slasher on knees, pull at the
doctor's waist to draw out the tooth. Father Christmas leans on
his broom and watches.)

Father Christmas:
   Look, look, ladies and gentlemen; more like a horse's, ele-
   phant's or a camel's tooth than a Christian's. Why, it would
   carry a quarter of beans across a rough, rocky road and never
   drop one.

Doctor:
   Fetch my pills, Jack.

J. Vinney:
   Fetch 'em theeself, then.

Doctor:
   What's that?

J. Vinney:
   Just a'coming, sir.
                  (Runs to get them.)

Doctor:
   Ladies and gentlemen, these are the most wonderful pills in the
   world. I cured Jack Giggins' wife with one of these yere small
   pills; she done no more than she done no less and after that
   she died it took nine blind men to lower her down through
   the roof of the house in case she should fall and break her
   neck.
            (Doctor then gives King George a pill.)

C

Doctor:
Fetch the medicine.

J. Vinney:
Shan't, fetch it theeself.

Doctor:
What's that?

J. Vinney:
Just a'coming, sir.
(Runs to get it.)

Doctor:
Ladies and gentlemen, this is Garland's blood mixture;
It will fetch a man back to life in a few seconds;
Apply a spot to his brow and a spot to his heart.
Arise, King George and fight thy part.
(King George jumps up.)

Beelzebub   (comes in a threatening attitude, club on shoulder,
frying pan in hand):
In come I, Beelzebub,
On my shoulder I carry my club;
In my hand the dripping pan;
Don't you think I'm a jolly old man?
Now then you yellow asses and black faces, can't you agree?
Last Christmas Eve I turned the spit;
I burnt my finger and felt it hit;
A spark flew over the table
And the pot lid beat the ladle;
King Jack stood up like a noble man,
Said he'd fight the dripping pan;
The dripping pan with his long tail
Swears he'll take you all to jail.

Fiddler Wit:
In comes I, Fiddler Wit,
With my great yud and little wit;
Me yud so big, me wit so small
I brought my fiddle to please you all.

What tune, ladies and gentlemen?
Oh, the old favourites!
Ran Tan, the tinder box;
Jack up the orchard;
Cat in the fiddle bag.

All sing 'Darkies lead a happy life' while the collection is taken
in the frying pan.

It is more usual for St George to kill the Turkish Knight, but
otherwise the play follows tradition closely. The Snowshill Morris
and the Snowshill Swedish were also danced on St Barnabas' Day.

The Robin Hood plays were less common in the Cotswolds than
elsewhere but the *British Calendar Customs* Volume III has discovered a chance mention of them in a seventeenth-century manuscript in Copenhagen University library. It is an account of two
Danes visiting England in 1652. They visited Enstone on 21 June,
where they found the rustics celebrating games '*quos sua lingua
Rabben hüt vocaliunt*'. These games would be the beginning of the
Midsummer celebrations, though Robin Hood was more commonly
associated with May Day. Midsummer was one of the times when
magic was practised, the gathering of fernseed for invisibility and
the sowing of hempseed to see one's future husband – both supposed to be attended with a certain amount of peril. Midsummer
was the date of the feudal fair in Burford. The charter was granted
in the fourteenth century and lasted for 15 days, seven before St
John's Day and eight after. The Midsummer Eve procession was held
in the middle of it and the Church Ale, the ancient forerunner of
church fêtes. The Midsummer fair was a hiring fair or 'mop' as
well and continued until 1914. It was held in Sheep Street. The
carters, shepherds and ploughmen came to it, each wearing something to indicate his profession, a wisp of wool for the shepherd
and a whiplash for the carter. The girls came too, in print frocks
and sun-bonnets. Those who accepted the earnest of a shilling were
considered bound to stay their year.

July and August pass without any notable festivals in the
Cotswolds, but September is rich in them. From 11 to 17 September
was formerly the date of the Wychwood Forest Fair, which will be
dealt with in Chapter 6. Painswick in Gloucestershire has a double
celebration. The 99 yew trees in its churchyard – for that is traditionally their number, though actually they have increased – are

clipped on 19 September and on the Sunday next after that the
Church-Clipping ceremony is performed. The children encircle the
church and dance. A service with a special hymn is given before.
This ceremony was a very old one in more places than Painswick
and more countries than England. Perhaps it has survived here by a
kind of pun because of the yew clipping.

'Puppy-dog pies' were eaten in Painswick on Clipping Sunday.
These were plum pies with a little china dog in each. Meat pies
would do but the dog was obligatory. The local tradition of the
origin of puppy-dog pies is that the ceremony of Church-Clipping
drew such a crowd of strangers to the place that the landlord of the
inn, desperate for meat to feed them, served up pies made of puppy
dogs. The china dogs are no longer sold in the shops and the pies
are not to be had at the local inns but Mrs Rogers of Painswick, who
has lived there all her life, says that they are still baked by her
daughters and grandchildren and that the china dogs they use are
hereditary in the family.

Holy-Rood Day, 14 September, was the date for nutting and at
North Leigh as elsewhere the Devil was likely to make one of the
party, particularly if the 14th fell on a Sunday. At Avening in
Gloucestershire where the church was dedicated to Holy Cross, the
feast was kept on the first Sunday after 14 September. Refreshments
were carried up to the ringers in the belfry and the fare eaten was
pig's head and apple dumplings.

Round Michaelmas time was popular for fairs. Burford's second
fair, granted by a charter of Henry VII, was held then and was
immensely popular. A pale shadow of it still lingers. Stow Hiring
Fair was held on the first Thursday before Old Michaelmas Day
and Chipping Norton held its fair on the day before. It was also
famous as a horse fair.

The Martinmas fair at Deddington was celebrated by 'pudden-
pies'. Christina Hole reports on Pudden-Pie Fair:

The November, or Martinmas, Fair at Deddington was called
Pudden-Pie Fair, because pudden-pies were made and sold then.
They had a very hard suet crust and were filled with boiled plum
pudding. The tradition said that a certain King once travelled
from Woodstock to Banbury, receiving gifts of local produce on
the way. Woodstock gave him leather gloves, Banbury its famous
light cakes. Deddington gave him something between the two —
pies meant to be eaten and yet resembling leather.

It sounds not unlike Scotch bun, eaten round Hansel Monday time.

Hallowe'en, the witches' night, was less observed in the Cotswolds than in the North or West. Guy Fawkes bonfires were of course popular with the young but there seem to have been no customs peculiar to the Cotswolds. The same is true of St Nicholas's Day, though in Oxford the Lord of Misrule was chosen then. St Thomas's Day, 21 December, was more generally observed, particularly in the Gloucestershire parts of the Cotswolds. It was called Thomasing, Gooding or Mumping and was the day on which old people were given small gifts of money to help towards their Christmas dinner. It was not thought of as begging. At Winchcombe children as well as old people were given small sums of money. At Aston Blank they asked for corn for their frumenty and at Todenham, near Moreton-in-Marsh it was the children who went from house to house and were given money, cakes and sweets. In general however 'Thomas so grey' was the patron of the old people.

St Thomas's Day was a foretaste of Christmas but the Christmas season began in earnest on Christmas Eve, when the houses were decked with holly and the Christmas log was dragged in and lighted. It was thought unlucky to bring holly into the house before Christmas Eve. In many parts of the Cotswolds the wassailers went round on Christmas Eve and they were followed by the carol singers. Many of the songs collected in the Cotswold area by Cecil Sharp were Christmas carols. In Partridge's ' *Collectanea* of Cotswold Place-Lore and Customs' in *Folklore*, 1912 we have a note on the wassail bowl.

Wassailers still go round at Randwick, Woodchester, Avening, Minchinhampton, the outskirts of Stroud, and probably many other villages. They formerly had a large wooden (maple) bowl, which at Minchinhampton was kept during the year in the possession of one man known as ' King of the Wassailers.' It was decorated with evergreens and small dolls. The latter are now omitted, and a modern bowl is used, with quite a bower of greenery and coloured paper over-arching it. Money is dropped into the bowl, and spent on drink. An old woman of seventy-eight can remember when there were as many as twenty of these wassailers in Minchinhampton; now there are but three or four. She says that there was never more than one band of them in a village.

The Minchinhampton song ran:

Wassail, wassail all over the town,
Our bread is white, our ale it is brown;
Our bowl is made of the mapling tree,
To my wassailing bowl I drink unto thee.
Here's health to our master and to his right eye,
God send our master a good Christmas pie!
A good Christmas pie that we may all see,
To my wassailing bowl I drink unto thee. . .

Here's health to my master and his right ear,
God send our master a barrel of good beer! . . .

Here's health to our master and to his right arm,
God send our master a good crop of corn! . . .

Here's to our master and to his right leg,
God send our master a jolly fat pig! . . .

This description of the bowl makes one think that the Buckland bridal bowl of which mention will be found in Chapter 12 must once have been used for wassailing.

Christmas Eve and the Twelve Days following it was the great season of the mumming plays and almost every village seems to have had its band of mummers.

In Tiddy's *Mummers' Plays* Christmas plays from Shipton-under-Wychwood, Leafield and Lower Heyford are included. The list published in *English Ritual Drama* is much longer but since this is primarily a catalogue of folk plays no specimens are included from the area. In Gloucestershire the following places are cited: Bisley, Blockley, Bourton-on-the-Water, Bussage, Chipping Campden, Dursley, Icomb, Longborough, Nailsworth, North Cerney, Northleach, Sheepscombe, Sherborne, Snowshill, South Cerney, Stroud, Tetbury, Weston-sub-Edge, Winchcombe and Wotton-under-Edge. In Oxfordshire we find Bloxham, Burford, Chadlington, Chipping Norton, Deddington, Great Rollright, Leafield, Shipton-under-Wychwood, Souldern and Upper Heyford. Most of these are Christmas plays. A full version of a summer mumming play which was probably also acted at Christmas has already been given but it would perhaps be of interest to include a mutilated fragment acted at North Newington before the First World War, which was published by Christina Hole in the *Annual Record of the Oxford-*

shire and District Folklore Society in 1956. It is given without
dramatis personae.

> In comes I old Father Christmas,
> Am I welcome or am I not.
> I hope old Father Christmas
> Will never be forgot.
> A handful of money and a cellar full of beer
> We'll welcome we and my company here.
> A room, a room I do require.
> Step in Jack Finney and show your face like fire.

Who do you call Jack Finney? My name is not Jack Finney.
My name is Mr John Finney, and if you call me Jack Finney
again, I'll chop you up as small as flies, and send you to the
cookshop to make Mince Pies.

> In come I, the noble doctor.
> How come you a doctor?
> I came all the way from Slaughter
> To fight for the Queen of Egypt's daughter.
> Who is the Queen of Egypt's daughter?
> I am the Queen of Egypt's daughter.

At this point the doctor tries to find out what is the matter with
Jack Finney, who has a face like fire. He pretends to draw a tooth,
and while doing so speaks the following words:

There was an old woman who had been dead seven years, buried
eight, in her grave nine. I cured her, and she had only one tooth
in her head, and that was as long as a Poplar Tree.

> Here comes I, old Belbug.
> On me shoulder I carry me club.
> In me hand a dripping pan.
> Don't you think me a jolly old man?

> In comes I, big Billy the sweep.
> All these young men I have to keep,
> Big and little, great and small.
> I think myself the best man of all.

> In comes I, who has never been yet,
> With my great head and my little wit.
> My head is big and my wit is small.
> I'll play you a tune that will please you all.

The words and the song that followed this were forgotten.

In this fragment one can make out the play pretty clearly. The entrant from Slaughter was almost certainly St George, the other combatant was, unusually, Jack Finney, with whom St George fought for the King of Egypt's daughter, generally a man-woman. The doctor should have come in after the combat, and then Beelzebub, to tidy away Jack Finney. Billy the Sweep probably had dolls hanging round him and Big Head and Little Wit came at the end to play, as he did in the Snowshill version. The things remembered and forgotten are instructive.

These mummers' plays went on through the Christmas season but there were some days to which special customs and beliefs were attached. Girls wanting to know their future husband would bake a dumb cake on Christmas Eve. The cake must be made in silence; the girl pricks her initials on it and sets it to bake in the ashes, leaving the door open. At midnight her destined husband is supposed to walk into the room and prick his initials on the cake beside hers. She must then consume it.

Cattle and stock were given an extra supply of food on Christmas Eve and at midnight the bees were supposed to sing in the hives. On St Stephen's Day little birds were shot and horses and cattle were bled as medical treatment. Holy Innocents Day, 28 December, was an unlucky day; a muffled peal was rung in many of the churches and no enterprise must be begun that day. It was, on the other hand, a day for children's parties and in some places the children were allowed to play in church. On New Year's Eve or on Twelfth Night apple trees were often wassailed, though the ceremony was more impressive in Worcestershire – the orchard county. A song sung to the apple trees at Upton St Leonard's near Painswick was published in Volume XXII of *Folklore*, 1911.

> Blowe, blowe, bear well,
> Spring well in April,
> Every sprig and every spray
> Bear a bushel of apples against
> Next new year's day.

In some parts of Gloucestershire as in the West Country it was believed that the cattle knelt in their stalls at midnight on Old Christmas Eve. Everywhere Twelfth Night was a time of general festivities. The Twelfth Night cakes became more and more magnificent in the nineteenth century; it was a time for masques and fancy dress. The Twelfth Night King and Queen were chosen by a bean and a pea baked in the cake. There was a last swing of revelry before Distaff Day and Plough Monday when work was taken up again after the long holiday. And so the New Year took its course.

3 Songs, Dances, Games and Rhymes

THE COTSWOLDS and the surrounding counties were great places for songs, dances and music. It is no accident that many of the churches have musicians carved round the towers or on the pillars. Cecil Sharp made his richest collection of songs in the West Country, Somerset, Devon and Dorset but he collected many songs in Oxfordshire and Gloucestershire too, and found perhaps his richest collection of Morris dances in this area. Headington and Bampton, outside the Cotswold area, trained the most famous Morris dancers but many were to be found in the Cotswolds, and were indeed discovered by later researchers. As for songs, Alfred Williams in his *Folk-Songs of the Upper Thames*, though he naturally writes chiefly of the Thames Valley below the Cotswolds, also explores the upper tributaries and gives us the words, though unfortunately not the music, of 30 songs from the lower Cotswolds. Some of them are ballads or well-known folk songs but some have a flavour of the drawing-room ballad. One that was a favourite with the Morris dancers, and was sung by Robert Baxter, the last of the Morris Men of Eastleach, has something of this flavour:

> When I sit by myself at the close of the day,
> And watch the blue twilight turn amber and grey,
> With fancies as twinkling and vague as the stars,
> And as distant as they from this life's petty jars —
> I know not, I think not where fortune may be,
> But I feel I am in very good company.

This strikes one as one man's composition with little trace of traditional rounding and shaping.

On the other hand we have from Charles Hope of Filkins an unusual and entertaining version of Gossip Joan, and we have such ballads as 'Fair Eleanor and the Brown Maid', 'The Draggle-Tailed Gipsies', 'The Shepherd's Daughter', 'Turpin and the Lawyer', 'The Golden Vanitee', and there are jocular tales like 'I went into the Stable', on the same plot as the Scottish 'Hame cam' oor Gudeman at Nicht', 'When shall we get married?' and 'Shepherd, come home to thy Breakfast', a more adult version of the singing game, 'Lazy Mary, will you get up?'. An interesting song which belongs especially to Gloucestershire is 'George Ridler's Oven' which is supposed to be a cryptic Royalist song, the property of the Gloucestershire Society, founded in 1657 to work for the Restoration of the Monarchy. George Ridler was supposed to be Charles I, the oven his party, the three singers who sang bass, mean and treble were the three orders of the estate, and so on, though some of the references remain unexplained. The song is sung in a strong Gloucestershire accent and if the interpretation given to it is correct its popularity seems to show that the country people of the Cotswolds were strongly Royalist — however Puritan the towns may have been.

Mrs Groves, in her *History of Shipton-under-Wychwood*, quotes from her father, George Pratt Hambidge, the titles of some of the songs commonly sung in Burford in his youth. He gives the first verse of one:

> First Miss Mary and then Master John,
> See how they do trip it along,
> See how he lands her over the stile,
> See how he kisses her all the while.

This sounds as if it might be the beginning of a song about a folk-dance processional, a dance which differed from the Morris processional in including men and women. The others are: 'Sweet Alice Benbolt', 'Under a tree with a bowl on her knees/Mary sat silently, shelling green peas', 'Kiss me quick and go my honey', 'Green grow the rushes, oh!', 'Oh come with me my Phillis dear/To yon blue mountain side', 'Sweet dreamland faces', 'The Miller and the Maid', 'Come out, 'tis now September', and 'Goodnight to you all, and sweet be your sleep'.

It is apparent that these songs, like those collected by Alfred Williams, consisted of a mixture of old folk songs and drawing-room ballads. There are also songs that belong to particular places and particular occasions, such as the Randwick Wap Song mentioned in Chapter 2.

Oxfordshire, Gloucestershire and the Cotswolds were, however, more remarkable for Morris dancing than for songs. Bampton and Headington are out of the Cotswold area but Chipping Campden is almost equally remarkable for a steady tradition of Morris dancing which has never needed to be revived and has always been in local hands. Some of the tunes have been borrowed from Longborough, which is equally notable and which has done some good revival work in neighbouring villages but the steps and figures are native to Chipping Campden. The fool and the hobby-horse still play their parts. The hobby-horse has not got the snapping jaws of the hooden horse of Kent. The head is rather small and dark-brownish, almost looking as if it was made of leather.

Some Morrises still survive, or have been revived; others are only retained in the memory of some older men. In John Kibble's collection of traditional material now lodged in Woodstock County Museum, there is a useful account of the way in which the Charlbury Morris dancing was organised:

From my earliest days I was hearing of the Morris dancing that had used to take place at Whitsuntide and other festive occasions.

Six or eight active men dressed in knee breeches, white stockings and low shoes, with bells fastened about their legs, waving handkerchiefs danced to music from a 'Wittle and Dub' or 'Tabor and Fife' as the whistle about a foot in length, together with a small flat drum, hung on the performer's finger, and beaten with short drum stick, was called.

The man in charge of the Morris, who carried the collecting box and conducted matters generally, was called the 'Fool', he kept the crowd back, flourishing a stick with a bladder tied on one end, and a calf's tail tied on the other, cracking jokes and generally adding to the fun.

He was the only man who had a wage. He had to keep his head, not drink too freely, so the others paid him to keep things straight, whilst they danced.

On one occasion Charlbury Morris agreed to pay the 'Fool' thirty shillings for the week. When the pay day came and he received the money, knowing the dancers, now their week's capering was over, had only empty pockets, tired limbs, and owing to the quantity of drink consumed, aching heads, said to them, 'Who is the fool now?'

The whole business got so steeped in drink and debauchery generally it seems that it went out.

At Enstone towards the end, the Morris was trained out of sight, in Cling Clang Lane, the trainer 'pum pumming' with his mouth, for them to get the steps, so an Enstone man told me.

Excellent work in the encouragement and preservation of local Morris dancing is done by the Cambridge Morris Men who made a summer dancing tour of the Cotswold villages. In April 1949 they published a booklet on the traditional dancers of the Cotswolds. I am indebted for an opportunity of consulting it to Mrs Cook of Bledington, the daughter of George Hathaway of the Bledington 'old side', who helped to train the 'young side'. Mrs Cook has a photograph of him carrying the old heart-shaped box in which the money was collected. The pamphlet contains so much useful information that I am reproducing a large extract from it (with the kind permission of the Cambridge Morris Men):

Traditional Dancers and Musicians
Ever since the first Tour of the Travelling Morrice in 1924, when the dances were taken back to the places where they belonged, members of C.M.M. have endeavoured to get into touch with surviving dancers and musicians of the traditional sides, both during tours and at other times, and in this way they may claim to have carried on Cecil Sharp's work. Some of the results of these inquiries have already been published. In addition to the dancers and musicians mentioned below, considerable time has, by

members of the C.M.M., in company with others, been given to verifying the Headington dances from William Kimber and the Bampton dances from William Wells.

Bledington

CHARLES BENFIELD (Bould). Fiddler of the old Bledington side, who helped to train the 'young' side. Tunes collected from him (1924), etc.) include *Over the Water, Saturday Night, Young Collins, Billy Boy, Bonnets So Blue, Highland Mary* and *Balance the Straw*.

JOHN HITCHMAN (Bledington). Squire and Tomfool of both old and 'young' Bledington sides. Died 27 November 1929, aged 79.

GEORGE HATHAWAY (Stow-on-the-Wold; formerly of Bledington). A member of the 'young' Bledington side. The Travelling Morrice learnt *Hey Away* from him at Maugersbury Manor, 26 June 1929. Gave much valuable information about details of the dances and help in verifying the tunes. Possessor of the old heart-shaped Bledington collecting-tin, which he lent to the Travelling Morrice during the whole of their tour in August 1946. Died 29 September 1948.

WILLIAM KERRY (Didcot; formerly of Bledington). A member of the 'young' side. Visited while living at Headington, Oxford, by Russell Wortley and Arthur Peck.

WILLIAM ROBERTS (Small Heath, Birmingham; formerly of Bledington). Another member of the 'young' side. Visited by Lionel Bacon.

RICHARD BOND (Idbury). Dancer and musician. Several dances and tunes were learnt from him, including a version of *Young Collins* (1924).

ALEC FRANKLIN. Brother of Henry Franklin. Alec was not a member of the side, but was 'a pretty dancer'. Dances learnt from him (Aug.–Sept. 1925) were *Mrs Casey, Old Woman tossed up, Ladies Pleasure, Princess-royal,* and *The Nutting Girl*. Died 27 December 1927, aged about 77.

MR PRATLEY. An old dancer. Seen in 1924, and again in 1931 (then aged 84).

WILLIAM DORE. Musician. Played us *Jockie to the Fair*, which his father used to dance. Mentioned to us Mr Ferriman, as one who knew all the tunes, but it was never possible to get into touch with him. Died during the 1939–45 war.

JOSEPH DORE. Perhaps an old dancer; witnessed our performance in 1937; he was then aged 96.

JOHN COOPER (Leafield; formerly of Chadlington). His father had been Squire and Fool of the Chadlington Morris. He taught the clap behind the back of the head in *Mrs Casey* and criticised the manipulation of the sticks in *Young Collins* (1945 and 1947).

At Stow in June 1931 the Travelling Morrice met Mrs Sherborne, aged 80, whose father Mr Busby, had been fiddler to the Fieldtown Morris.

Longborough

HARRY TAYLOR. Fiddler and Foreman of the Longborough Morris. Dances learnt from him (June 1924) were *Saturday Night, Cuckoo's Nest, Old Trunkle* and *Old Woman tossed up in a blanket*. Died 1931, aged 87.

GEORGE JOYNES. Fiddler. Never played for the Longborough side, but learnt some of the tunes from Henry (or Tom) Taylor, Harry Taylor's eldest son, and gave copies of them to the Travelling Morrice in 1924.

HENRY HATHAWAY (Lower Swell). He used to dance in the Longborough side when it was led by Harry Taylor. He said we should have a Fool with bladder and cow's-tail. Was aged 74 when he saw us dance in 1933.

NED HATHAWAY (Stow-on-the-Wold). Danced no. 2 ('off-side foremost') in the Longborough side. Died about 1932.

ALBERT TOWNSEND. The dance-tune *Highland Mary* was learnt from him in June 1924. Died 1929.

JIM SIMPSON (Battledown, Cheltenham; formerly of Sherborne). He taught the double-clap before the half-hey in the *Monk's March* (June 1938). Died 1941.

THOMAS PITTS (Eastleach; formerly of Sherborne). Musician and dancer. Sang us several of the Sherborne tunes (June 1938).

CHARLIE JONES (Sherborne, formerly of Windrush). Probably a member of the last Little Barrington and Windrush side.

Oddington

CHARLES ('MINNIE') TAYLOR (Church Icomb). A member of the Oddington side, and a very famous dancer. Also knew the Bledington and Longborough traditions. Danced *Jockie to the*

Fair and *Princess-royal* and taught *Highland Mary* and a leap-frog dance to the tune of *Swaggering Boney* (1924 and 1929). Died 31 December 1929, aged 93 or 94.

There is an article by Manning in *Folklore* Volume VIII on Morris dancing and the instruments used to accompany it, which is of interest as an earlier record and there is a further article in Volume XL of the same periodical.

Most of the traditional social dances which have survived to modern times are those described as 'longways for as many as will', though Sellenger's Round was still danced on May Day in several places. The commonest dances were 'Bonnets So Blue', 'Nancy's Fancy', 'The Triumph', 'The Flowers of Edinburgh', 'Brighton Camp', 'Three Meet' and 'The Soldier's Joy'. Some places had dances of their own. Of these one of the best documented is 'The Snowsle Swedish', collected by Cecil Sharp in 1909 and again noted in 1930. Before this Mrs Newman of Snowshill learnt it from an old fiddler. It has not been danced since the last war but Mr and Mrs Meadows were kind enough to hum the air for me and indicate the formation. It is a version of 'Three Meet'. It will be remembered that Mr Meadows was Father Christmas in the Snows-hill mummers play. A lively solo dance called 'Bacca Pipes' – a kind of sword dance over crossed churchwarden pipes – was performed by men.

The sports that were common all over the country were practised also in the Cotswolds. Some of them have been mentioned in Chapter 2 under Captain Dover's Games. There were cock-pits in a number of the inns, though cocking was sometimes considered a disreputable sport, not so much for its cruelty as because of the disreputable company which it attracted. Burford Races on the Downs were famous in the seventeenth century. Hare-coursing was common on the wold and badger-baiting was practised, as the anecdote in Chapter 11 shows. Cock-shying was a schoolboy sport and belonged chiefly to Shrovetide.

Almost every inn throughout the country had a skittles alley but Oxfordshire claims Aunt Sally as a special sport. It is supposed to be old but possibly it took the place of cock-shying. An article in the *Evesham Journal* of 3 March 1967 gives the rules. Most people will remember the Aunt Sally often played at bazaars and fêtes – a black doll with a clay pipe in her mouth. The object of the thrower was to break the clay pipe. The Oxfordshire Aunt Sally played in pub gardens was rather different. She is a round piece of wood, with a roughly marked face on it, set on a metal stand. Each player has six sticks about the length of a rolling-pin and his object is to knock the head off six times without touching the stand. Each hit counts one. There are eight players on each side, so that the total score for each 'leg' could be 48. There are three legs. For a match there is an umpire and someone to replace the fallen head. The winners in 1967 were the Black Horse team of Salford near Banbury. The game is commoner in Oxford than in the Cotswolds, where there are many places that have not heard of it. A Burford friend said that he sometimes played it as a lad but there are said to be almost 50 teams in Oxford and they claim there that it dates from the fifteenth century. It seems that it may be rather a newcomer in the Cotswolds.

George Swinford gives an account of the games played in Filkins and the neighbourhood in his youth or in the memory of his elders. All of them seem now extinct.

Old Sports at Filkins

About sixty years ago there were four inns in our village, and three of these had quoits-beds, where the men used to play in the evenings. These beds were made by digging two holes, about two yards square and one foot deep, and then filling them up with clay. They were about twenty yards apart, with an iron peg stuck in the centre. We boys used to have a penny each for watering the beds and covering them with sacks when the weather was hot and dry.

Each player had two steel quoits, about 6 inches in diameter and weighing about 2lbs. The object of the game was to drop the quoit as near as possible to the peg. If it fell right over the peg, it was called a ringer, and counted two points; the next nearest counted one. Quoit-playing was once very popular in Filkins, but it finished about 1900.

Another well-liked game in those days was called Bandy. It was something like hockey, and was played with sticks and a ball called a nunney. We used to cut our sticks from the hedges, and if possible, we chose one with a little bend on the bottom, like a hockey-stick. The nunney was a block of wood, preferably tough elm, about the size of a hen's egg.

To start the game the players all met and chose two captains.

D

These then picked their followers, one by one, till all were in one team or the other, and the nunney was then taken to the centre and hit off by one of the captains. There were no goals, and the nunney was knocked from hedge to hedge, or from wall to wall, as the case might be.

We had no rules or regulations, except one. This was that if an opponent covered the nunney in any way with his feet or body, we all shouted 'Turn, Bumby!' If he did not get out of the way at once, we could hit him, and you can guess what this often meant! We had always to be on the look-out for the police or the farmers, and sometimes we had to go two or three fields away if either turned up. Bandy has not been played since the first football came to the village in 1898.

Marbles was a great game in Filkins when I was a boy. I have often seen old men playing it. One variety was called Ring Tall. A ring was made in the dust, and each player put a marble, called a cot, upon it. Then all stood on a line about three yards back and bowled. A marble called a tall was put on the thumb-knuckle and held there with the forefinger. By flicking the thumb it could be made to travel a long way, and it was wonderful to see how straight and far some of the men could shoot. You had to keep your hand on the ground while shooting. The rule was 'Knuckles down: all four fingers touch the ground'.

The player nearest the circle shot first at the cots, and if he hit one and knocked it out of the ring, he could claim it. He then went on shooting until he missed, after which the next man could shoot at one if he liked. If he hit it, its owner was out of the game, but the tall did not have to be given up. The game ended when all the cots were knocked out of the ring.

Another form of Marbles was Follow Tall, which was played along the wheel ruts in the roads. Men used to play it going to work and boys going to school. Only two played at a time. The first man put his tall in the rut and the other shot at it. If he hit it, he received one cot, and then the second man had his turn, shooting at his opponent's tall. As long as you kept your tall behind, you could go on shooting, winning a cot for every hit.

Then there was Knock-off, which was played against a wall. Each player put a cot on a line drawn about six inches from the wall, and then, in turn, tried to hit the cots from about two yards away with a large marble called a flump. Whatever cots a man knocked off the line, he claimed; but if another player chose to aim at his flump and hit it, he had to give up all he had won, and was then out of the game.

Shin-kicking used to be a popular way of fighting. Robert Prior, of Pear Tree Farm, told me when I was a boy that formerly the men of the village used to settle any dispute by kicking each other's shins. They used to soak their boots in rainwater and dry them in the sun to get them hard for the purpose. I have heard this talked about by other old men, but nothing of the kind is known now in Filkins. I think it must have died out about a hundred years ago.

This shin-kicking game was also practised in Berkshire at the Uffington games. 'Kick-shins' it was called and was the carters' sport. They held each other by the lapels of their coats and kicked at each other's shins with iron-tipped boots. The loser had to pay for the drinks. The most famous champion shin-kicker lived in Lambourne in 1870. His legs were twisted and deformed by the wounds he had received. Rowlands in the seventeenth-century verse 'Letting of Humor's Blood in the Head Veine' (1606) seems to hint at the same sport in the line: 'To try it out at foote-ball by the shinnes' – but perhaps he combines shin-kicking with football, which was an almost lethal game at the time.

Girls' games were much gentler than boys'. Flora Thompson gives us an idea of the singing games which were played even by 12-year-olds in her hamlet just beyond the edge of the Cotswolds. Sometimes they would sing as they danced but on other evenings they would play singing games, most of which are still familiar. 'Oranges and Lemons', 'London Bridge' and 'Here We Go Round the Mulberry Bush' are known to everyone. Rather more unusual is the acting game 'Here Come Three Tinkers, Three by Three', or the plaintive 'Isabella, Isabella, Isabella, Farewell', or 'Here comes an Old Woman from Cumberland', or the medieval castle song of 'Waly, Waly Wallflowers', or the song of magic and divination, 'Sally, Sally Waters'. Flora Thompson says that unsuspected depths of dignity and drama were stirred by these songs and the players became for a time transformed. Versions of all these can be found in Lady Gomme's *Dictionary of Singing Games*.

Short, doggerel rhymes served many purposes. Some were gnomic proverbs, some were weather and seasonal rhymes. The greater part dealt with localities, some descriptive but more were vituperative. The place rhymes, descriptive or abusive, chiefly concern us at the moment.

The three beautiful churches near Banbury, which are linked together by tradition as having been built by three brothers with an anonymous assistant who turned out to be the Devil, are linked together by a rhythmic verse:

> Bloxham for length
> Adderbury for strength
> And King's Sutton for beauty.

Bloxham and Adderbury are too near together to be friendly. Adderbury people say:

> Bloxham dogs
> Come to Adderbury to buy your togs.

Bloxham people are nearly all fair. About 1935 an enquirer, wondering if the hostility was accounted for by a racial difference, asked a Bloxham man if the Adderbury people were dark. The Bloxham man replied, 'I never looked at 'em long enough to notice.'

A somewhat similar rhyme is given by Flora Thompson as directed by her village against the Hardwick children:

> Old Hardwick skags!
> Come to Fordlow to pick up rags
> To mend their mothers' pudding bags,
> Yah! Yah!

Banbury is the subject of many rhymes. Everyone knows:

> Ride a Cock Horse
> To Banbury Cross
> To see a fine lady
> Ride on a white horse.

In the 1790 version the 'fine lady' is called 'an old woman', which led to the notion of making her a witch in the pantomime *The Witch and the White Horse* performed at Astley's Royal Amphitheatre in 1833. However, the rings on her fingers and bells on her toes suggest a ceremonial festival which may well have inflamed the Puritans of Banbury to destroy the great cross, described by Leland as ' a goodly cross with many degrees about it '. At any rate it and all the other crosses about the town were destroyed in Queen Elizabeth's reign, in 1601 or a little earlier. The zeal of the Banbury Puritans was a by-word. Braithwaite in ' Drunken Barnaby's Four Journeys ' applies the well-known story of the Sabbatarian who hanged his cat for killing a mouse on Sunday.

> To Banbury came I, O profane one!
> Where I saw a Puritane-one
> Hanging of his cat on Monday
> For killing of a Mouse on Sunday.

The people of Banbury seem to have had a kind of spite against beauty as the next rhyme about them shows.

> Dirty Banbury's proud people
> Built a church without a steeple.

The old church in Banbury was said to be one of the most beautiful in the Cotswolds – almost a cathedral. From 1773 to 1780 it was surveyed four times and pronounced fit to stand for ages, yet in 1790 the vestry voted to have it destroyed, which was done with great difficulty because of the solid Norman work. It took days to burn and a new church was constructed at enormous expense.

In Elizabeth's reign the crosses were torn down; in Charles I's the castle was blown up; in the time of the Georges the church was burned down and in the nineteenth century the town sold its regalia.

An unusual butter rhyme collected by the Oxfordshire Folklore Society mentions a mysterious character, the great Bull of Banbury:

> Come, butter, churn,
> Come, butter, come.
> The great Bull of Banbury
> Shan't have none.

Other opprobrious rhymes are:

> It is allowed
> That Stroud
> Holds naught that's pretty,
> Wise or witty.

And

> Stow-on-the-Wold
> Where the wind blows cold
> And the cooks have nothing to cook.

Or

> Hailey, Crawley, Curbridge and Coggs,
> Witney spinners and Ducklington dogs,
> Finstock on the hill, Fawler down derry,
> Beggarly Ramsden and lousy Charlbury.

Or in the same strain but terser

> Beggarly Bisley, Strutting Stroud,
> Mincing Hampton, Painswick Proud,

or

> Woodstock for bacon, Bladon for beef,
> Hanborough for a scurvy knave
> And Coombe for a thief.

Other places have single epithets, such as 'Drunken' Deddington, which is really a tribute to the beer brewed there. Coombe, as
well as its reputation for being a nest of thieves, is called 'Silly'
Coombe and has two of the wide-spread numskull stories attached to
it. It is said that they packed manure round the church tower to
make it grow. Rain washed away the top layer of manure during the
night and in the morning the parishioners called out to each other,
'Look, ee's growed!' They were also credited with the feat of pen-
ning the cuckoo to keep on the spring. This, together with the
accusation of being thieves, suggests the possibility of their being
forest people planted there — that is an alien population. Leafield
was equally despised and feared by Charlbury.

In the same spirit George Swinford remembers that the Filkins boys used to call after anyone from Broadwell:

> ' Broadwell scrubs
> Born in baskets and christened in tubs ! '

and then take to their heels. The pattern seems the same everywhere.

4 Historical Traditions

To TOUCH ON the historical traditions of country so rich in history as the Cotswolds is to have a hundred difficult decisions to make. In choosing the subjects to dwell on I have tried to put the emphasis on the tradition rather than the history but this is of two kinds; oral tradition may be the source of history, or the folk memory may play around material with either a documented or a literary source. I have already referred to some prehistory in the legendary stories of the Rollright Stones and the Hoar Stone at Enstone. There is a curious trace of the work of tradition on what must at first have been purely literary history. Occasional farms scattered all over Britain are called 'Troy Farm' or 'Troy Town'. There is one between Somerton and Fritwell on the doubtful edges of the Cotswolds. The origin of the name is curious. The trace of a maze is always to be found near these 'Troy Towns'. The received history of Britain learnt by schoolboys in Elizabethan times went far

back beyond the Norman Conquest. It was to be found in Nennius,
Orosius and the suspect writings of Geoffrey of Monmouth and
from these sources reached the pages of Holinshed. According to
this received history Britain was first colonised by Brut, the grandson
of Priam and the son of Aeneas, who, arriving here with his companion Corineus, after a victorious campaign in France, found the
country inhabited by a tribe of giants. They were conquered and the
two chiefs divided the island between them, Corineus taking Cornwall and Brut the rest. Corineus was especially the giant-slayer and
he wrestled with Goëmagot, the fiercest giant of all and threw him
into the sea over Taw Cliff. This was traditionally the origin of the
famous Cornish manner of all-out wrestling which was practised
for uncounted centuries and the giant figures borne annually in the
Lord Mayor's Procession were supposed to represent Gogmagog
and Corineus. In course of time the name Corineus passed out of
usage and the giants were called Gog and Magog. 'By Gog
and Magog' was a common oath of Cockneys till the nineteenth
century.

A further popular legacy of these Trojans was the Troy Game,
the treading of a maze cut out in the turf and supposed to follow
the ramifications of the Cretan Maze or of the ancient Crane Dance.
Everyone will remember the allusion to it in *A Midsummer Night's
Dream*:

> The quaint mazes in the wanton green
> For lack of tread are undistinguishable.

The maze at Troy Farm is about 400 yards long and ends in a
central loop.

It is more probable that these mazes came from the Roman
occupation rather than from the British, for the game was played
in the Circus Maximus in Rome at the opening of the *Ludi Apolli-
naris* and was alluded to by Virgil and by Pliny. These mazes may
well have been cut and used by the Roman colonists, who believed
themselves to be the descendants of the Trojans as much as ever
the British could have done. From Roman times onwards sympathy
was always with the Trojans rather than the Greeks and Hector was
more esteemed than Achilles. We should consider the whole com-
plex entirely founded on the ascendancy of the classics in education
had it not been for this curious feature of the name given to the
mazes and to the farms which preserved them. The adjective

'wanton' in Shakespeare's lines seems to suggest that these dances had some connection with fertility rites – but perhaps that is to push conjecture too far. In the frontispiece of *Annalia Dubrensia*, the booklet devoted to the celebration of Captain Dover's Games, there is an elaborate square – rather like an Elizabethan herb garden – which one guesses to be a representation of a maze for the Troy Game, and such indeed it was, for Aubrey mentions that there was a maze on the Downs at Captain Dover's Games.

Not many traditions of the Roman villas or the Romanised way of life have survived until accident threw the knowledge in the way of archaeologists. Of the great Roman manors of Chedworth, North Leigh and the Palace of Woodchester no living tradition survived, although the Roman snails still inhabit the Chedworth woods and the ornamental Roman pheasants escaped from the terraces into the forests. Nettles and the beech tree are supposed to have been imported by the Romans and inscribed stones tell us the names of colonists and of local deities. But the spoken word has perished with the Latin tongue. Traditions of the Saxon invasion, however, linger everywhere. At Perrot's Brook near Cirencester are two lines of fortifications supposed to have been thrown up by the British as a defence against Cedric, King of the West Saxons.

Cirencester itself has a more circumstantial and romantic story, recorded again by Geoffrey of Monmouth with his unfailing eye for the picturesque. Alexander Neckam, the Abbot of Cirencester 1213–17, was one of the first to connect the story of the Saxon victories in the sixth century with Cirencester. Although he refers to Geoffrey of Monmouth's *Historia Britonum*, he probably had local tradition behind him. According to this story the Britons had regained Cirencester from the Saxons and held it for six years until the Saxons called up fresh troops, led by an African called Gormund who finally captured the town by an ingenious device. He caught a great number of the sparrows who nested in the thatched roofs of the town, fixed lighted straws to their tails and released them. They flew back to their roosts and set fire to the town in so many places that the garrisons could hold it no longer and were forced to retreat across the Severn. In medieval times the town was sometimes called *Urbs Passerum* because it had been conquered by sparrows. Why Gormund was supposed to be an African is a matter for conjecture. The name is Scandinavian and the destruction of a a town by fire-carrying birds is to be found in some Scandinavian legends. Possibly Gormund was supposed to be a magician and the association of Africa with magic accounts for his nationality. At any rate later writers ignore it.

The memories of the Cotswolds in medieval times are most lively when concerned with the hunting in Wychwood Forest. 'Old John', who used to drive the waggonette and afterwards the bus from Shipton station to Burford, would talk as if he had almost seen them of 'King John and King Charles, and those' who used to come hunting in the forest. Time meant little to him, for in the same breath he would talk of Sir John Reade and his heir, Wakefield the footman, whose story is told in Chapter 6, and go on to anecdotes of his own grandfather, a gamekeeper who had inadvertently killed a poacher. The most romantic and best known of the medieval legends, that of Fair Rosamund, is told in the next chapter.

A memory of the terrible times of the civil wars in King Stephen's reign, said to be the worst known in England all through the Middle Ages, survives in a tradition about the twelfth-century chapel of Postlip, near Sudeley. The present manor is a fine Elizabethan build-ing but a medieval manor stood on its site and the chapel, which had been used as a barn, has been repaired. The tale of its founda-tion is that in the times of Stephen the countryside was so dangerous that the lord's serfs and yeomen dared not attend the parish church and begged him to build one nearer, which he did. He must have been a good and considerate lord. An interesting feature is a tiny window high up in the south wall of the nave in which 'the poor soul light' used to be put in medieval times, to remind the neigh-bours to pray for the souls of the dead and especially, one may suppose, for those who were too poor to pay for masses. The windows are uncommon, for the practice ceased before the Reforma-tion.

The spectacular episode at Cirencester in which the rising of the legitimist peers and the attempted rescue of Richard II was quenched has, curiously enough, taken little hold on the popular imagination in spite of the fight between the citizens of Cirencester and the royal dukes, Kent and Salisbury, who were Richard's half-brothers, and their illegal execution after the victory. The townspeople profited in the affair not only by the spoil they took but by the subsequent favour shown them by Henry IV, who stood by them as well as he could in their disputes with the abbot of Cirencester and also granted the coveted right of a guild-merchant, an honour which in the event proved too difficult for them to handle. Within a few years the abbot had got back his toll rights and in 1416 a new abbot got the right of guild-merchant. Perhaps this final failure effaced the earlier success from the popular mind but the memory of it may have contributed to the zeal with which the abbey was destroyed at the Reformation and the Parliamentary bias of Cirencester during the Civil War.

Hints and rumours of Dick Whittington hang over Gloucestershire but the only place in the Cotswolds that can really claim a connection with him is Coberley Manor near Seven Springs and this is a splendid example of the way in which folk fiction can play pranks with history. The foundation of Coberley's claim to Dick Whittington is that Sir Thomas Berkeley of Coberley married the widow of Sir William Whittington of Pauntley who brought her small son with her. Local tradition goes further, however, and claims that Whittington was born at Coberley and that one of the defaced effigies in the church represents him and his cat. However, though all agree that he was born in Coberley, everyone points to a different house. The more authentic story mentions a stone caryatid discovered in the fifteenth-century town house of the Berkeleys, which represents a small boy carrying a cat. This is now in the Guildhall Museum in London. Unfortunately for both these stories the article by James Tait, following Lyson's analysis of the story in the *Dictionary of National Biography*, says that Whittington's mother was Sir Thomas Berkeley's widow when she married William Whittington, that his father was outlawed when he was born – probably for marrying Lady Berkeley without permission – and that the figure in the Guildhall is carrying an unrecognisable animal. Furthermore, Sir Ivor Fitzwarryn, Whittington's father-in-law, was never a merchant. After that it is anyone's guess – but at least we know that tradition has been busy.

Wherever castles and great nobles were to be found the Wars of the Roses left its mark. Unlike the Wat Tyler and Jack Cade risings it was a nobles' and not a people's war but wherever battles are fought and castles are sieged the poor suffer, though through the Wars of the Roses the burgesses managed to keep their prosperity and even to rise in status. The Cotswolds had some connection with these wars. Warwick the Kingmaker was lord of the manor at Burford and it was in Wychwood that Elizabeth Woodville is said to have met and captivated Edward IV. But the closest connection with the Wars of the Roses comes at the very end. Minster Lovell, where the true Cotswolds begin, was the home of the friend and minister of Richard III, Francis Lovel. The manor at Minster

Lovell had been built by his grandfather on the site of a small priory attached to the Norman abbey of Ivry. It was one of the unfortified manor houses of the fifteenth century, built while times were still peaceful. Francis Lovel had been the playfellow of Richard of Gloucester at Middleham Castle in their boyhood and when Richard acquired the throne Lovel rose with him. He was one of the men most odious to the Lancastrians. He, Ratcliffe and Catesby were the subject of the couplet that everyone knows:

> The Cat, the Rat and Lovel the Dog
> They all ruled England under the Hog.

As long as Richard remained in power all was well with Lovel but when Richard was defeated and killed at the Battle of Bosworth bad times came. Lovel raised a revolt in the North of England which nearly succeeded but not many people wanted the war to drag on and Lovel was forced to escape to Flanders to the court of Richard's sister, the Duchess of Burgundy. There he met a young lad, Lambert Simnel, born near Minster Lovell, who claimed to be the Earl of Warwick, Clarence's son, and took up his cause. In May 1487 he landed in Lancaster and marched to York, where Richard III had been beloved. His force consisted of Irish foot soldiers and German mercenaries and few Englishmen indeed came to join him. They were defeated at Stamford Bridge and Lovel was last reported swimming his horse across the Trent and failing to get foothold on the steep bank. It was believed, however, that he made his escape to Flanders and hid there in obscurity. There was one rumour that the body of a man in armour was found wedged in a hollow tree, from which the weight of his armour prevented him from escaping. It is said that there was a rumour round Minster Lovell that he had come home and was in hiding somewhere. Whether this was of later growth it is impossible to say, for in 1708 the Clerk of the House of Commons reported that workmen repairing a chimney in Minster Lovell Manor had broken into a small secret room and found the body of a man sitting at a table with a book in front of him and a dog at his feet. This they saw for a few moments and then, as the fresh air blew into the room, the whole crumbled into dust. There is no corroboration of this, but the authority of the House gained it instant credence and most people believed that this must have been the body of Francis Lovel. It was dogmatically stated that he had stolen home and that the secret of his presence was known only to one faithful servant, who kept the key of his hiding place and fed him. The servant was taken ill and died and Lord Lovel was left to starve.

This hiding place and its discovery has drawn another tale into its circle, the wide-spread story, 'The Mistletoe Bough'. It will be familiar to everyone: the story of a young bride on her wedding day playing hide-and-seek and hiding so well that she was never found. After days of searching they came to the conclusion that she had eloped with some more favoured lover, but years later someone opened a chest in a disused attic and found inside it a skeleton in bridal rags. The chest had a catch lock and had shut down on her. This tale is told about the Copes of Bramshill, a vicar's daughter in Somerset and the Lovels in Derbyshire. This last is the best documented and the name Lovel, in combination with the discovery of a skeleton, has attracted the tale to Minster Lovell. A song, 'The Mistletoe Bough', written in the nineteenth century was very popular at village concerts and has spread the story all over England and to the United States.

Tradition remembers a good deal about the sixteenth century, both the sweeping away of the monasteries, the persecutions under Mary Tudor and the reign of Queen Elizabeth I.

Painswick holds the memory of a lord of the manor even more hated and feared than Burford's Laurence Tanfield, Sir Anthony Kingston, a kind of sixteenth-century Judge Jeffreys. He was zealous to further King Henry VIII's purposes in the Reformation and was rewarded with the manors of Miserden, Quenington and Flaxley in addition to his hereditary manor of Painswick. He led a thousand Gloucestershire men to suppress the Pilgrimage of Grace and in Edward VI's reign went down to Cornwall to repress the Western Rebellion of 1549. Holinshed tells the story of the cruel trick which Sir Anthony played upon the mayor of Bodmin. The mayor had forwarded the rebellion but when it had been put down he pleaded that he had acted under constraint and his friends thought that they had managed to make his peace:

But howsoever it was, Sir Anthonie Kingston that was provost-marshall in the kings armie under the lord privie seale wrote his letter unto the said maior signifieing him that he and other with him would come and dine with him such a daie. The maior seeming to be glad thereof, made the best purveiance he could to receive them, and at the time appointed Sir Anthonie Kingston

came with his companie, and were right hartilie welcomed of the
maior. But before they sat downe to dinner, calling the maior
aside, he told him that there must be execution doone in that
towne, and therefore willed him that a paire of gallowes might
be framed and set up with speed, so that they might be readie by
that time that they should make an end of dinner.

The maior with all diligence caused the same to be doone; so
that when dinner was ended, Sir Anthonie calling the maior to
him, and asking whether the gallowes were set up accordinglie
as he had willed, the maior answered that they were readie.
Wherewith Sir Anthonie taking the maior by the hand, desired
him to bring him to the place where they stood, and comming
thither and beholding them, he said to the maior; Thinke you
maister maior that they be strong inough? Yea sir, quoth he, that
they are. Well then said Sir Anthonie, get you even up unto them,
for they are provided for you. The maior greatlie abashed here-
with, said; I trust you meane no such thing to me. Sir said he
there is no remedie, ye have been a busie rebell, and therefore
this is appointed for your reward: and so without respit or staie,
there was the maior hanged.

There is a pitiable spectacle on both sides here: the poor timid
mayor obsequiously erecting the gallows that could only be intended
for his late associates and Sir Anthony violating all the laws of
hospitality and refusing that time to make his peace with God which
was considered so necessary at that period.

On his return from his expeditions Sir Anthony proceeded to
practise at home the qualities he had developed in the North and
West. The Enclosures Commission of 1549 was very unpopular
and was met by rioting and the tearing down of fences. Sir Anthony
erected a gallows upon Sheepscombe Green and a prison in Painswick; and what was more he gave three estates, one to maintain
gallows, one to have ladders always in readiness and the third to
provide halters. He also provided that the tithing man of Sheepscombe should be hangman. Rudder, writing in the eighteenth
century, says 'There are many people now living who remember
the gallows, and the tithing man for the time being still enjoys a
piece of ground there called Hangman's Acre, but in this respect
his office is a sinecure.' This curious legacy lends credibility to a
story which has always seemed unconvincing in Laurie Lee's *Cider
with Rosie* about the Hangman's House. *Cider with Rosie* is set in

the Stroud area. It is possible that the Hangman's House related to Sir Anthony Kingston's Hangman's Acre at Sheepscombe.

A curious legend about Queen Elizabeth was invented and propagated by one man, Thomas Keble, the vicar of Bisley and John Keble's nephew. His father Thomas Keble, who was vicar before him, seems also to have been interested in the manufacture of traditions, for it was he who adapted the Derbyshire well-dressing customs to the Seven Springs of Bisley. Workmen who were building the new village school near Over Court – where Queen Elizabeth is supposed to have stayed as a child – found a medieval stone coffin containing the bones of a young girl. From this Thomas Keble built up a theory that the little Elizabeth had died at Bisley and that her hosts had been too much afraid of Henry VIII to confess her death to him. They looked for a substitute and the only child like her in looks and equally intelligent was a boy, and so the boy of Bisley became eventually Queen of England – and could never marry. A complementary story about the little Dauphin, the son of Louis XVI, which was founded on the fact that a banker's daughter called 'jilting Jenny' was discovered when she died to have been a man in disguise, may have suggested the legend to Thomas Keble. Wildly improbable as it is, one still occasionally meets people who believe it.

Woodstock Palace, pulled down to make room for Blenheim, had a wealth of traditions, beginning with Fair Rosamund. Henry II had the first of his serious quarrels with Thomas à Becket when they were staying at Woodstock, one of a series which ended only with Becket's life. It was at Woodstock that Elizabeth endured the most dangerous and tedious of her imprisonments as a girl, when she was suspected of complicity in Wyatt's rebellion. She was allowed neither pen, inks nor books and it was here that she wished she could change places with the milkmaid whom she heard singing so pleasantly.

Near to Woodstock is Ditchley Park, the home of old Sir Henry Lee whose character is vividly described by Scott – though misdated by nearly a hundred years. Henry Lee was truly an Elizabethan but he received visits from James I and his sons and in 1605 was given leave to enclose part of Wychwood for a private house, and here for 300 years was his herd of red deer, with white fallow deer amongst them, which gave rise to a legend of ghostly deer haunting Lord Dillon's park. A pleasing story of Sir Henry Lee is that of Bevis, his mastiff hound, whose portrait inscribed 'More faithful than favoured' hung in the dining room at Ditchley for almost 300 years. The story behind the picture is that one night Bevis insisted, against his custom, on sleeping in his master's room. He was turned out several times but always came back, until Sir Henry allowed him to stay. In the middle of the night there was a tremendous growling and Bevis flung himself on an unseen intruder. When a light was brought he was found to be holding down Sir Henry's valet, who confessed that he had meant to murder and rob his master. After that Bevis was favoured as well as faithful.

When we come to the seventeenth century and the time of the Great Civil War, traditions are so many and so lively that one can only choose a few of them.

We should perhaps begin with Broughton Castle, where the inception of the war was engineered with great subtlety and secrecy. One can still see the little room where the conspirators met, high up and approached by a stair that has access to no other room. It was guarded by one faithful servant and no one else knew who came; but if that man had played false and the conspirators had been arrested the government would have rounded up in one swoop Pym, Hampden, Vane, Lord Brooke, Warwick, Best and Essex— the cream of the malcontents, for in those days Cromwell had not yet come into prominence. As the war went on Lord Say and Sele began to think that he had sown the wind and reaped the whirlwind. He went into retirement when Cromwell came to power and in the end was active enough over the Restoration to secure not only pardon but place. Just before the Restoration he painted his great drawing-room white. King Charles was the White King, and white was in those times a token of Royalist sympathies. It is said that at King Charles's execution the citizen's wives of London let their white petticoats show below their dark gowns as a token of mourning.

Edgehill, the first great battle of the war, is for that reason particularly memorable. We have many oral descriptions of it, among them that of James II, then a schoolboy. We have many too in oral tradition. One recorded by H. A. Evans is of three traditional anecdotes from a man over 70 who heard them from his grandmother, who lived to be over 90. She heard them from her grandfather, who was a boy when the battle was fought. According to tradition Cromwell was watching the battle from Burton Dassett Tower and when he saw how the Parliamentary cavalry were being routed he slid down the bellropes and led his own troop in flight.

E

The account of the ghosts of Edgehill will be mentioned in a later chapter.

Another supernatural appearance, which has, however, a naturalistic explanation, is that of the Devil of Woodstock. In the October and November of 1649 the Commissioners of the Long Parliament occupied Woodstock Palace, turning the royal dining-room into a wood store, into which the wood from the uprooted King's Oak of Woodstock Forest was carried. Their nights were made hideous by sounds and experiences closely resembling poltergeist manifestations. They are generally supposed to have been engineered by a lively Royalist, Joe Collins, and a band of friends but were sufficiently convincing to frighten the Commissioners away. Thomas Widdows the clergyman of Woodstock wrote a pamphlet, *The Just Devil of Woodstock, or a true Narrative of the several Apparitions, the Frights, and Punishments, inflicted upon the Rumpish Commissioners.* This is recapitulated by Robert Plot in his *Natural History of Oxfordshire.* The emphasis laid upon the sacrilegious uprooting of the King's oak is significant in this account.

There are innumerable tales of individual sufferings and escapes. Charles II's escape from Worcester is the subject of many of them. Tradition gives him almost as numerous hiding places as the beds occupied by Queen Elizabeth. Among them is one attached to Painswick Beacon. Just below it is a farm called Paradise. The story is that Charles spent a cold, draughty night on the Beacon and when he was received in the farm below it he thought himself so well off that he called the place Paradise—and so it has been named ever since. It is difficult to fit this anecdote into the carefully documented diary of the King's flight but it is a pleasant anecdote for all that.

Another escape-from-Worcester story is that of Arthur Jones of Chastleton. He was a fugitive from Worcester and after 30 miles of stiff riding he arrived worn out and stabled his tired horse. But he had hardly started a meal when his pursuers arrived on his heels, believing that they were pursuing the King. Fortunately Chastleton was supplied with a secret room out of the best bedroom and Arthur Jones at once took refuge in it. The troopers suspected from the horse that the fugitive was close at hand but they searched the house in vain and finally decided to stay—unfortunately in the best room with only a very thin partition dividing them from the fugitive. A cough, a sneeze, even an imprudent movement would be fatal. Lady Jones offered to bring up some supper for the troopers. She laced their wine well with laudanum and soon they were sound asleep.

Arthur Jones stepped carefully over them, selected the best horse in the troop and rode away to safety. After a time he came back and lived secretly in one of the cottages.

Chastleton was always Royalist in sympathy. Juxon, who was a near neighbour, held secret services there when the use of the prayer book was forbidden and finally left them the Bible which the King had given him on the scaffold. It is in Chastleton House still. The parlour was painted white for the Restoration and is still white. In the eighteenth century Chastleton House was the centre of the Jacobite group in that part of the Cotswolds and has as fine a set of Jacobite glass as any in the country.

After the Restoration Burford was much visited by Charles 11 for the races on the Downs and particularly beloved by Nell Gwynne. Her eldest son was given the title of Earl of Burford. The story is that Nell Gwynne was sitting with her baby in the Priory when she said, ' If you don't give this brat a title I'll throw him out of the window' and made the motion of doing so. Half alarmed for the child and half laughing the King exclaimed ' I'll call him Earl of Burford '—and that was his title. There were gay times in Burford after the Restoration but there were sober people among the burgesses who gave a better welcome to William 111 than Tory Oxford did—and a handsomer present too.

Life was pleasant to the more cultured of the country gentry as the eighteenth century wore on. Lord Bathhurst of Cirencester is an example of the cultured gentleman of his day. Among his friends were Congreve, Pope, Swift, Gay and Prior, not so deep or learned a company as Lord Falkland gathered round him at Great Tew but brilliant and delightful for all that. Maria Edgeworth, who was born at Black Bourton, gives us a good picture of the society at the end of the eighteenth century. Things were not so good for the country people, whose lot was growing harder as enclosures deprived them of their common lands and garden plots and made them increasingly dependent on their scanty wages. The Chartist Riots at the beginning of the nineteenth century have left many traditions behind them of those bitter times and things did not improve, in spite of efforts made to improve education in the country, until the campaign of Joseph Arch began to be effective. Mrs Groves has given a vivid account of the way in which this affected some of the women of Milton at the end of the century:

A very striking incident happened in Ascott in May, 1873.

Because the men on one farm joined the union they were ' given the sack ', viz., dismissed, and two men from Ramsden were engaged instead. Some sixteen women from the village approached the said men, requesting them to desist from work, which they readily did on learning the circumstances of the others leaving. The farmer took the matter up by summoning the women before the local magistrates at Chipping Norton, who, showing something of the class spite of the time, convicted the women to seven or ten days respectively. Religion was well represented on the convicting side, two clergmen sitting on the bench, one of them leaving at his death some time afterwards nearly a hundred thousand pounds.

These convictions caused such resentment in the district that thousands assembled in Chipping Norton threatening riot if the women were not released, so they were removed to Oxford at midnight to serve their sentence. On the completion of their time they were welcomed home and, on the village green, Joseph Arch made a presentation of £5 to each woman, which had been subscribed for such purpose.

Names are omitted in this matter, as some of the families concerned, but not responsible are still living, and these hard and unchristian things are better forgotten. It is interesting to know that one of the women mentioned was still living in Milton [May 1933], sixty years after the event.

One can only touch on a point here and a point there in this rapid review of all remembered centuries. The most significant aspect of it is to see what lives in remembrance and what is forgotten.

5 Tales and Legends

TALES, LEGENDS AND ANECDOTES of all kinds are to be found all over the Cotswolds – historical traditions, saints' legends, ghost stories, witchcraft anecdotes, tales of robbers and sheepstealers and jocular tales and anecdotes. Many of these will appear in their appropriate chapters but some are so detailed and articulate as to deserve inclusion in their own right. One of the Cotswold saints, St Kenelm of Mercia, is buried in Winchcombe, though he met his death in the Clent Hills in Worcestershire.

Winchcombe, already inhabited in Neolithic times, and with fine Roman remains, rose to greater importance under the Saxons and became the capital of Winchcombshire in the Kingdom of Mercia. In 788 good King Kenulf founded a great abbey there for 300 monks. Two years later he died, leaving behind him two daughters and his little seven-year-old son, King Kenelm. The older sister, Quendreda, was a wicked and ambitious woman who coveted the crown for herself. So she persuaded her lover, Ascobert, to take the boy out hunting in the Clent Hills and murder him there. It is said in the legends that the child knew by a dream the fate that was intended for him and went willingly. Though 'small in age' he was 'great in mind and piety' and died reciting the *Te Deum*. While they rested after the chase Kenelm fell asleep and Ascobert began to dig his grave. As he was doing so the child woke up and said: 'This is not the place ordained for you to kill me. Look, I will plant this stick and it will blossom at once as a token.' He stuck a little ash twig into the earth and at once leaves sprang, the black buds burst and the dark flowers came out. But Ascobert's heart was untouched by the miracle. He took the child out of the forest indeed but before they reached home he cut off his head and buried it with his body under a thorn. In an instant a white dove sprang out of the head and flew away. It flew all the way to Rome and dropped a scroll at the Pope's feet. On the scroll was written in Anglo-Saxon script:

> In Clent Cow-pasture under a thorn
> Of head bereft lies Kenelm, King born.

The Pope and his cardinals were unable to decipher the scroll but an Englishman present translated it and the Pope sent an order to Wilfred, the archbishop of Canterbury, to make a search for the body. It was found, with a long knife beside it, under a thorn bush high up on Clent pastures, through the persistent lowing of a white cow, and was carried over to Winchcombe to be buried beside King Kenulf. Where the body had lain hidden in Clent a holy spring burst forth and a chapel was afterwards built beside it. On the way up Sudeley Hill to Winchcombe the body was set down for a short time and here again a holy spring marked the place. As the body was borne solemnly to the minster Quendreda stood at the palace window reading the psalter backwards for some evil purpose. As the hearse passed, her eyes started out of her head and spattered the page of the psalter with blood. The legend of St Kenelm was not written down till the eleventh century when it was recorded by Florence of Winchester and Geoffrey of Monmouth. It was clearly in oral circulation long before, for the shrine of St Kenelm was much resorted to and many miracles recorded. There is no mention of the murder, however, in the *Anglo-Saxon Chronicle* and Quendreda afterwards became abbess of Southminster. In the sixteenth century Leland, in his *Itinerary*, tells us that the boy was buried at the east end of the church beside his father. In 1815 there was a curious confirmation of this. The abbey church had fallen into ruins after the Reformation but the foundations were excavated in 1815 and two stone coffins were found at the east end with the bones of a grown man and a child in them and beside the bones of the child lay a long knife. The bones and the knife crumbled when exposed to the air but the two stone coffins are preserved in Winchcombe church.

Long Compton is just in the Cotswolds and its close association with the legend of the Rollright Stones makes it interesting to note a very different legend about the place, recorded, curiously enough, in the chronicles of the Yorkshire abbey of Jervaulx, as late as the reign of Edward III. It is a legend of St Augustine, the missionary to the Saxons. In the course of his missionary journeys St Augustine travelled through Oxfordshire and Warwickshire and visited the little town of Long Compton, where the priest complained to him that the lord of the manor refused to pay tithe of his possessions and though the priest had threatened him with excommunication, he could do nothing with him.

Augustine called the lord up to the altar rail to expostulate with him and found him as stubborn as the priest had said, so, as he moved up to the altar to perform the mass, he cried out in a loud voice: 'Let all those who are excommunicate leave the church.' The lord left the church but as he reached the churchyard there was other movement there, for a gravestone was lifted up and a dead man came out and began to move away. Augustine called on him to stand and made him tell his story. He had been a Briton, he said, and the Saxons had come and set a Saxon priest over the parish; because he would pay no tithe to the invaders he had been excommunicated and so had died. Augustine told him to point out the grave of the priest, raised him, and told him to absolve the man who had resisted him. Ghost absolved ghost and they both returned to their rest. The lord of the manor and all the congregation had listened in awe and terror to this colloquy and the lord submitted himself humbly to the bishop and was ever after a faithful child of the Church.

This story well illustrates the mingling of Briton and Saxon in the Cotswold area, perhaps all the more because it was recorded so late.

In various parts of Britain – and scattered through Europe as well – there are legends of underground caverns in which there are sleeping warriors, who can be roused by appropriate action. These

can be the followers of Arthur, Charlemagne or Frederick Bar-
barossa, or they can be mysterious, unspecified characters such as
were guarded by the wizard of Alderley Edge. Sometimes the
caverns contained strange treasures or mechanical or magical figures
somewhat after the style of Friar Bacon's brazen head. Often there
is a mysterious, ever-burning light, such as that supposed to be found
in an underground pagan temple in Rome. The legend of Tor-
Barrow Hill near Cirencester is similar. Rudder quotes it from one
of the Bodleian Rawlinson Papers written by William Budden and
printed in 1685:

> Two men digging a gravel pit at the foot of this hill, having
> sunk four yards deep, discovered an entrance into the hill, where
> they found several rooms with their furniture, which being
> touched, crumbled to dust: In one of them were several images
> and urns, some with ashes, others full of coins, with Latin inscrip-
> tions on them. Entering another, they were surprised at seeing
> the figure of a man in armour, having a truncheon in its hand,
> and a light in a glass like a lamp, burning before it. At their first
> approach, the image made an effort to strike, so at the second
> step, but with greater force; but at the third it struck a violent
> blow, which broke the glass to pieces, and extinguished the light.
> Having a lanthorn, they had just time to observe, that on the left
> hand (I suppose of the figure) lay two heads embalmed, with
> long beards, and the skin looking like parchment, when hearing
> a hollow noise like a groan, they hastily quitted those dark apart-
> ments, and immediately the earth fell in and buried all the
> curiosities.

The legend of Fair Rosamund escaped from the pages of history
and gradually built itself up into a picturesque tale of love and
jealous hatred. Rosamund Clifford, born about 1140, was the
daughter of Walter de Clifford, and the mistress of Henry 11, by
whom she had two children, William Longsword, Earl of Salisbury and Geoffrey, bishop of Lincoln. She was lodged by Henry in
his palace of Woodstock and finally retired to Godstow nunnery
where she died. Henry's wife, Eleanor of Aquitaine, was much hated
in England, and popular tradition soon cast her for a villain's role.
Ralph Higden of Chester was the first chronicler to give Eleanor a
part in the drama and to introduce us to the maze of 'Rosamund's
Bower'. His account was somewhat enlarged by Stow:

Rosamund, the fayre daughter of Walter Lord Clifford, concubine to Henry II (poisoned by Queen Elinour, as some thought) dyed at Woodstocke (AD 1177), where King Henry had made for her a house of wonderfull working; so that no man or woman might come to her, but hee that was instructed by the King, or such as were right secret with him touching the matter. This house after some was named Labyrinthus or Dedalus worke, which was wrought like a knot in a garden, called a Maze; but it was commonly said that lastly the queene came to her by a clue of thridde, or silke, and so dealt with her that she lived not long after; but when she was dead she was buried at Godstow in an house of nunnes, beside Oxford, with these verses upon her tomb:

> *Hic jacet in Tumba, Rosa Mundi non Rosa Munda.*
> *Non redolet, sed olet, quae redolere solet.*
> (Here lies in the tomb the Rose of the World,
>   not the Clean Rose.
> She stinks now, who used to smell so sweet).

This savage epitaph might almost have been written by Eleanor herself. Curiously enough, Leland records that when Rosamund's tomb was opened at the Dissolution of the Monasteries:

> Her bones were closid in lead, and within that bones were closyd yn lether. When it was opened, a very swete smell came owt of it.

Fair Rosamund has a place in Michael Drayton's 'Heroicall Epistles' and Percy included Deloney's Ballad of Fair Rosamund in his *Reliques*. Here the maze is described as a quaint and solid piece of masonry:

> Most curiously that bower was built,
>   Of stone and timber strong;
> An hundered and fifty doors
>   Did to this bower belong:
>
> And they so cuninglye contriv'd,
>   With turnings round about,
> That none but with a clue of thread
>   Could enter in or out.

> And for his love and ladyes sake,
>   That was so faire and brighte,
> The keeping of this bower he gave
>   Unto a valiant knighte.

However, these precautions were of no avail, for Henry was forced to go to France to put down his sons' rebellion and, after a reluctant farewell, he committed Fair Rosamund to the care of the knight and set sail. Then Eleanor came into action:

> For when his Grace had past the seas,
>   And into France was gone,
> With envious heart, Queene Ellinor
>   To Woodstocke came anone.

> And forthe she calls this trustye knighte
>   In an unhappy houre,
> Who, with his clue of twined-thread,
>   Came from this famous bower.

> And when that they had wounded him,
>   The queene this thread did gette,
> And wente where Ladye Rosamonde
>   Was like an angell sette.

> But when the queene with stedfast eye
>   Beheld her beauteous face,
> She was amazed in her minde
>   At her exceeding grace.

> ' Cast off from thee those robes,' she said,
>   ' That riche and costlye bee;
> And drinke thou up this deadlye draught
>   Which I have brought to thee.'

Rosamund's prayers and promises of amendment were naturally unavailing and she was forced to drink the potion.

In later tradition Queen Eleanor was supposed to offer Rosamund the choice between being poisoned or stabbed and ' the dagger or the bowl?' became an almost proverbial expression. Until the eighteenth century extensive ruins of what was supposed to be Fair Rosamund's

Bower remained in Woodstock but they were destroyed when the Duchess of Marlborough built Blenheim Palace.

The whole Cotswold area is full of ghostly traditions of spectral coaches and black dogs but for the most part these are mere records of appearances, sometimes ending with the laying of the ghost – as at Wilcote and Burford – but seldom telling a consistent tale such as those told in Somerset, Shropshire and the North of England. Mrs Haynes, who was one of the Wallers of Burford, with a ghostly tradition of their own, had a story of a spectral coach at Whittington, where her grandparents lived in the manor in her childhood. The occupant of it was Sir Laurence Tanfield. The lane along which he drove was called 'The Wicked Lord's Lane' and it was believed that whoever saw the ghostly coach would die. Fortunately not everyone could see it. Mrs Haynes told me that once, when she came from her school in Cheltenham to visit her grandparents, the groom who drove her told her that the Wicked Lord had been seen and that he himself had been the first to find the victim. He had seen him lying at the roadside covered with a rug, when he went out to exercise the horses. What had happened was that a stranger had engaged the local waggonette to meet him at the station and, sitting up beside the driver, had been taken suddenly ill. The driver could not hold him up and drive, so had laid him down by the roadside, covered with a rug, and gone off for help. By the time the groom saw him he had died. The groom and most of the village were convinced that he had been killed by the sight of the Wicked Lord. More will be said of these ghostly coaches in the chapter on supernatural beliefs.

Black dogs are scattered fairly widely over the Cotswolds and are of different kinds; some of them human ghosts, some of them doggy and some evil spirits. One on Birdlip Hill is a helpful spirit who guides lost travellers. Ruth Tongue however heard of another visitant on Birdlip Hill, the Devil. She heard the following tale from a groom in Cheltenham in 1926:

There was a shepherd above Birdlip Hill, and there was Old Nick on the road to catch travellers. The shepherd wanted a potion for a sick ewe from the Inn far below.

He went afoot – horses and carts never went that road. Horses don't care for devils. So Old Nick was glad to see him pass. ' I'll have him on the way back,' says he.

The shepherd had a black jack there and his drinking-horn

filled to cheer him on the long uphill road, and he wrapped up
the sheep's medicine which smelt nasty and hot, and started off. Up
he goes and up till he comes to the turn near Black Dog's Lane.

He'd a notion Old Nick might be about there, so before he
passes it he has a swig of ale from the horn to hearten himself,
and pours back in some of sheep's tonic, well-boiled.

Then he goes on up.

Out comes Old Nick and grabs him. 'Ale!' says he. 'Good
brown ale.'

'Spiced for you, sir, special,' says the shepherd civilly, hand-
ing the horn, and taking to his heels.

Old Nick was in such a hurry to catch him that he gulped the
drink down first, and then it – the sheep tonic – caught him. They
heard him roar right away in Cheltenham.

He never goes near Birdlip Hill now!

A humorous twist to a story is common all over the Cotswolds.
One gets it even in the ghost stories; in the one, for instance, told to
Mr Frederick Bayliss by his father. Mr Bayliss senior was a brewer
and at the turn of the century he was living and working at
Chipping Norton but he was courting the woman he afterwards
married, who lived at Milton-under-Wychwood. So every Wednesday and Saturday he used to walk the five miles to Milton, spend
the evening with his girl and walk back. On Wednesdays he had to
get home in good time so as to start work early in the morning but
on Saturdays he could afford to stop later, so that it was often about
12 o'clock when he got to the two Sarsden pillars that stood on each
side of the track to Churchill as he turned on to the Chipping
Norton road. He didn't much fancy being there at that time of night
because he used to hear a sound like a coach passing him and coming
along the track that crossed the main road almost at right angles.
He was glad when one dark night he was joined by a companion.
This chap walked at his side, just a pace or so behind him, but near
enough to talk. He wasn't a talker though, but Mr Bayliss was and
he chatted away till they got to the Sarsden stones and the chap
turned the other way.

The same thing happened next Saturday. It was a dark overcast
night and Mr Bayliss was glad of the company. But the third Saturday it was a bright moonlight night. His companion came up behind
him again and Mr Bayliss started chatting away as usual. Then
suddenly he thought to himself: 'I don't believe I've ever heard

this fellow say a word.' And he looked over his shoulder. Then he
started off down the hill as fast as he could pelt, for walking just
behind him was an Elizabethan gentleman with a ruff round his
neck and nothing above it. He had a head right enough but it was
tucked firmly under his arm. Mr Bayliss knocked them up at Downs
Hollow Cottages and spent the rest of the night there. After that,
he set off early on Saturdays as well as Wednesdays and took good
care to be at the Sarsden pillars by 11 o'clock at latest. So he never
saw the ghost again.

Even the Puritan divines had their share of humour and readiness,
though not many of them would have been as quick-witted as the
Rev. John Dod, at one time rector of Hanwell near Banbury. At the
beginning of the Civil War he encountered four drunken Cavaliers,
who seized on him, stuck him up a tree and, knowing his repute as a
preacher, declared that he should not get down again until he had
preached them a sermon upon Malt. He began at once:

Beloved, I am a little man, come at a short warning – to deliver
a brief discourse – upon a small subject, to a thin congregation,
and from an unworthy pulpit.

Beloved, my text is MALT, which cannot be divided into words,
it being but one; nor into syllables, it being but one; therefore, of
necessity, I must reduce it into letters, which I find to be these;
M.AL.T.

M, my beloved, is Moral, A is Allegorical, L is Literal, and T is
Theological. The moral is set forth to teach you drunkards good
manners, therefore – M – is My Masters, A – all of you, L –
Listen, T – to my Text.

The allegorical is when one thing is spoken and another is
intended; the thing expressed is MALT; the thing signified is the
Oil of MALT, which you Bacchanals make, M – your meat, A –
your Apparel, L – your Liberty, and T – your Text. The literal is
according to the letter. M – Much, A – Ale, L – Little, T –
Thrift. The Theological is according to the effects it produces,
which I find to consist of two kinds. The First respects this life,
the Second, that which is to come. The effects it produces in this
world are in some, M – Murder, in others, A – Adultery, in all, L –
Licentious Lives, in many T – Treason. The effects consequent in
the World to come, are M – Misery, A – Anguish, L – Lamen-

tation, T – Torment. Thus, sirs, having briefly opened and
explained my *short* text, give me leave to make a little use and
improvement of the foregoing, and first, by way of exhortation.
M – my Masters, A – All of you, L – Leave off, T – Tippling.
Secondly, by way of commination – Or M – My Masters, A – All
of you, L – Look for, T – Torment.

At that he got down from his tree and went home in triumph.

It is not often that the preacher has the last word in humorous
anecdotes of this kind but it must be admitted that Mr Dod unwit-
tingly caricatured the type of sermon that was too often ground
out by the Puritan divines, in which each word of the text was tor-
tured into a heading and turned and twisted with various meanings.
In this brief example we almost get an epitome of the hour-long
sermons to which our ancestors listened with such serious attention.

Edward Rainsberry, the rector of Long Compton, has collected
several jocular tales of the district which are well-known elsewhere.
One has a variant in Somerset, 'The Man who answered the Owl':

> There is a story told about a Long Compton man, Tom Wyton,
> who talked to an owl in Whichford wood. Tom went to Rollright
> on Boxing Day, and after a good evening with his friends was
> making his way home. He thought he would take a 'short cut'
> through Whichford wood, and eventually reckoned he should be
> near the edge of it. As time passed, he realised that in fact he was
> lost and he began to shout, hoping that if he was near the road
> someone might hear him. At last he heard a voice, 'Who-o-o-o,
> who-o-o-o!' Tom shouted again, and back came the answer
> 'Who ar you? Who ar you?' 'I be Tom Wyton from Long
> Compton,' he replied to the owl.

The fools of the district are the Ebrington mawms. They are the
subjects of the same stories of mucking the church tower to make it
grow that are told about Coombe. The local rhyme about it went:

> Master Southam a man of great power,
> Lent a horse and cart to muck the church tower.
> They mucked the tower to make it grow high,
> But not as lofty as the sky.
> And when the muck began to sink,
> They swore the tower had grown an inch.

Another Ebrington man, on his way home from Ilmington one moonlit night, was missed by his companion and was found by the pond trying to fish out the great round cheese he saw there.

But the Ebrington men were sometimes sharp enough. One evening Walter Taylor, one of Mr Rainsberry's best informants, was in Ebrington pub when a stranger came in. 'What be the name of this place, then?' he asked. 'This be Ebrington,' replied the landlord. 'Oh, Ebrington, that be wheer all the fools live.' 'Well, I don't know that they all live here. We get plenty passing through!'

Bibury in the Colne Valley – now a too-famous beauty spot – has a jocular story attached to it. It is said that an Oxford student once offered to teach the landlord of the Swan Inn how to draw strong and mild ale out of the same cask. He drilled a hole near the bottom of the cask and told the landlord to stop it with his finger; then he drilled a hole at the top of the cask, which the landlord had to stop with his other hand. 'Oh, I've forgotten the spigots!' he said. 'Hold on a minute and I'll fetch them!' He went out of the inn, mounted his horse and rode away. The landlord was immobilised until he could get someone to relieve him and by that time it was too late to catch the practical joker. But the landlord had the best of it in the end. The story spread round and so many people came to laugh at him for his gullibility that his trade doubled.

Painswick, near Stroud, is noted for the purity of its air and the longevity of its inhabitants. It is this characteristic which makes it the appropriate subject of one of the international tale types 'The Oldest in the Farm'. The story is told both in prose and verse.

In the old, old days, they say, when men drank good spring water and didn't know what it was to smoke a pipe, a pilgrim was climbing up the hill towards Painswick when he saw an old, old chap squatting on a heap of stones and fairly crying his eyes out. 'What's the matter, father?' he said 'Oh, oh!' said the old man, 'Father's given me such a lathering!' The pilgrim thought the old chap was wandering in his head. 'No, no father,' he said. 'You oughtn't to be here on your lonesome. I'll give you a lift home.' So he hitched the old fellow on his back – he was no more than a morsel of skin and bone – and he carried him on till he came to a little farmhouse. 'This is home,' says the old chap, 'but I'm main feared o' father.' 'No, no your father'll not hurt you,' said the pilgrim and he knocked at the door. And the door was opened by an old, old, old man with his beard right down to the ground. He was in a tearing rage and he had a big ash stick in his hand. Well the pilgrim was a bit taken aback, but he said, ' Oh granfer, you'd not hurt this poor little old chap. He's crying something pitiful and he says you've been lamming him.' ' And why for shouldn't I lam him, bad boy that he is?' says the old man. ' Look at his poor old granfer up there in the tree, risking his old neck to pick us cherries, and this 'ere rascal's been a-dubbing of he with stones. Just let me catch 'im!'

At that the first old fellow scrambled down and ran, and the pilgrim he ran too, for he thought to himself, ' They live for ever at Painswick.'

A tale told by M. Shayler, now 26, as a child by an old man in Leafield is a good example of a nursery nonsense tale:

I were going along the road one night an' I seed a feller coming along towards me, and I thought it were 'ee and 'ee thought it were I. And we got a little closer, an' I knowed it were 'ee and 'ee knowed it were I. An' we got a little nearer, an' I were *sure* it were 'ee an' 'ee were *sure* it were I. An' us got a little closer still, and I were darned positive it were 'ee and 'ee were darned positive it were I. And we comed right up to each other, and it weren't neither of us!

A light-hearted fairy anecdote was collected at a rather far remove by Ruth Tongue. She heard it from a nurse in Middlesex Hospital, who had been told it in her student days by an Oxfordshire fellow-student, who in her turn had heard it from her grandfather, an Oxfordshire farmer, in about 1900. It was an anecdote of his own farm:

There was a lazy, hard drinker who never worked unless it was at harvesting time, when the farmer sent out a firkin for the labourers. Then he was the first to come hanging round out of his turn.

They used to send him right out mid-field under everyone's eye, but he sneaked back to the hedge if you weren't quick, for a sly swig. My grandfather's men got pretty tired of this, and hid the firkin, but he sneaked round and found it, and when they were all busy he ran off with it.

He'd got a good skinful already, so he made for the woods, and lay down on the turf-side of a mound that had a hawthorn on it – I said he'd already had a skinful, didn't I? Well he said that's what made him too drowsy to move.

Well, first he saw something small and green by the bank, then another, and then a whole crowd; but somehow he couldn't move. Then all of a sudden he was alone, and could, and he did.

He picked up the firkin for a long swig. 'Funny dream I had,' he said, 'all about nothing.'

And little voices all round twittered back at him, 'And that's what you'll find in the firkin!'

There have not been many mentions of the fairies in the Cotswolds since A. J. Evans, in the *Folklore Journal* of 1895, recorded that Will Hughes used to see them dancing round the King-Stone at Rollright but Ruth Tongue has uncovered one or two fairly well-authenticated tales. One about the Dursley district was told her by an English Folk Dance and Song Society member at Halsway Manor in 1970, and she had heard something of it from Gloucester correspondents in 1966.

One winter evening a traveller was riding across the wolds to Stroud to stay with friends, when the dusk came down and snow began to fall, thick and blinding. He felt himself quite astray and had begun to despair of finding any shelter for himself and his horse when he saw a light ahead, and pressed on until he found himself at an Inn. The door was open, a fire was burning inside, and a little, old groom came to his horse's head. He dismounted and the groom led the horse away to the stable. The traveller followed to see that his beast was well cared for, and found the ostler already hard at work. The horse was eating away at his oats with a pile of sweet hay beside him, while the groom busily dried off his snowy back and rubbed his cold ears. The old groom looked up with a smile, and the traveller made his way back to the Inn well pleased.

There was no one there and he stood warming himself by the fire until he heard someone moving upstairs. He went up, and was silently welcomed by a servant in a green livery, who showed him into a comfortable bedroom with a warm fire and a good meal set in front of it. He pulled off his boots, took his wet clothes to dry and gave him warm slippers. There was mulled ale keeping

F

hot by the fire. The traveller ate his supper, got into a great four-poster bed and fell fast asleep. He awoke however well before cockcrow, anxious to get to Stroud and set his friends' minds at rest. The fire had been made up, mulled ale was warming by it and there was bread and cheese on the table. He put on his dried clothes, ate his breakfast and went down, but he could find no one about. There was no one in the stable either, but his horse was ready for the road and still munching his breakfast. So the traveller went back to the Inn and put two guineas on the table.

The stars were bright and there was a thin covering of snow, but he soon got to Stroud, where his friends were relieved to see him, and said it would have been madness for him to try to get through the storm : ' I thought it best not to try to get through,' he said, ' so I stayed in that splendid Inn above Dursley. They made me very comfortable and my horse couldn't have been better looked after.'

' At Dursley!' his friend said. 'There's no inn at Dursley!'

' Indeed there is,' said the traveller. ' A queer place, but they looked after me all right. I didn't see anyone but the groom and a servant, but nobody could have looked after me better.'

' I told you so,' said his hostess to her husband. ' I told you there was an inn above Dursley.'

' I'd like to see it then,' he said.

' I'll take you back,' said the traveller, and they all three set out. ' That's not the way to Dursley,' said the host. ' Oh yes it is,' said the traveller. ' There's the track of my horse's hoofs. And look, I remember those trees. You'll find my inn just behind them.'

But there was nothing there but two gold guineas lying on the frozen snow.

' I've been told they come out on stormy nights,' said the lady. ' And they never take payment. They never stay after cockcrow. It's lucky you went early or you'd have waked in the snow.'

There are many tales, particularly Celtic ones, in which guests of the fairies have awakened to a cold lodging on the hill-side but few in which the lodging has been so harmless and so hospitable as in this fairy inn.

It is doubtful if the white kitten in the following tale was a fairy or not. It is one of the gipsy tales of the Wychwood Forest area. The hill road over the wold from Burford to Stow could be very danger-

ous in a cold winter. In the nineteenth century a small contingent of
soldiers billeted in Stow-on-the-Wold left it, refusing to believe that
it could be called Stow-in-the-Ole, and were lost in a snow-storm.
The same fate threatened a caravan of gipsies who were struggling
up the hill through a snow-storm one Christmas Eve. They were
brought almost to a standstill by the storm and they were scared of
the ghosts in the haunted wood near the forest. This wood must have
been the coppice near Idbury which has a name for being haunted
to this day. The gipsies called the ghosts 'Snow Foresters' and they
were all round the caravan, whining and screeching and pattering
on the window:

But one of the boys heard a mewing that was not the Snow
Foresters, and he opened the door a chink and let in a little white
kitten. 'Put it out!' said his mother, for white cats are thought
to be death-tokens by the gipsies. 'No Mam, it's as lost as us and
as little as me. Us can't turn it out. I do believe 'tis Christmas Eve
tonight, and if 'tis Christmas Eve 'twill speak to us, if us ask it in
rhyme.

> 'Is it, Kit-Cat?
> Tell us that.'

And with that the Kit-Cat speaks. 'So 'tis,' says the Kit-Cat, 'and
you'll all win safe through if ye can keep on to the church bells.
Hearken to the birds a-twittering and follow after them.' And
right above the sound of the white Snow Foresters they heard a
twittering of hundreds of little birds flying up to sing their
Christmas carol in Stow Church.

With that they all plucked up their hearts, and the horses
heaved up the van through the snow, and they sang all the carols
they could think of to keep the white Snow Foresters at bay, until
they came to a farm on the outskirts of Stow, and there a farmer let
them lodge for the sake of Christmas charity. The Christmas bells
were ringing and the snow stopped, and the little white Kit-Cat
was gone. 'She wasn't a witch's cat,' said the little boy, 'I think
she was a little fallen angel that was earning her way back to
Heaven.'

'Ah,' said the old Grannie by the fire, 'that was another Good
Deed for her.'

This was a tale belonging to Aaron Lee, a Wychwood gipsy in the 1860s, which was told to Ruth Tongue in Hertfordshire about 1941 by a family of gipsies on their way to Wales with several vans and ponies. There must have been many tales that could have been collected from the Wychwood gipsies after the enclosure of the forest land in the 1860s. Even so late as 1967 the Lees still believed that a fairy was a fallen angel that could win its way back to Heaven.

This small collection of tales gives some idea of the variety of themes which engaged the attention of the Cotswold peasants, though in these days, and probably at all times, the jocular tales were the commonest.

6 The Traditions of Wychwood Forest

THE NEW FOREST is a parvenu to Wychwood Forest, which appears to date from prehistoric times. Mr Groves of Shipton used to claim that the Leafield people, forest men who settled in Leafield when the forest was enclosed in 1862, were ancient Britons who had taken refuge in Wychwood Forest – they were certainly very different in type from the inhabitants of the surrounding countryside. Wychwood was a favourite hunting place for the Saxon kings and was taken over by the Normans. Henry I rebuilt a hunting lodge at Woodstock and made a park seven miles round, surrounded by a stone wall. He made a kind of zoo there with lions, tigers and the creature who excited the greatest interest, the porcupine which, according to tradition, shot its quills at the dogs that attacked it. The tradition of this beast was still alive in Shakespeare's time.

There are many references to Wychwood in the Court rolls of Henry III. Thomas de Langley was the chief forester in his time –

not always a very conscientious one, for he was fined £100 at the Court of Forest Pleas held in Oxford in 1229. His son John seems to have been just such another, for in 1305 he was fined 20 marks for forest offences. In 1218 there had been an order for the perambulation of Wychwood for the establishment of its ancient forests and the disafforestation of recent additions.

In medieval times grants of wood for building or fuel were often made to neighbouring monasteries or to nobles, as well as gifts of live deer or boars for stocking parks, or of venison. Many fines were imposed for stealing timber but these were lighter for the poor and were sometimes remitted altogether in cases of extreme poverty.

Wychwood was Crown property until, with Cornbury Park which adjoined it, it was given by Charles II to the Earl of Clarendon.

In 1792 the Commissioners of Woods and Forests made a detailed report on Wychwood – then almost entirely surrounded by a stone wall – that is mentioned below in Mr. Andrews's story of Millin's Oak.

Within the enclosure the land was divided into five walks, called Ranger's Walk, Roger's Hill, Patch Hill, Porter's Hill and South Lawn Walk. The actual Crown land was estimated at 3,709 acres. Three of the five keepers' lodges were on Crown land and two on the Duke of Marlborough's. The villages of Ascott, Asthall, Fulbrook, Minster Lovell and Swinbrook, as well as certain hamlets in the parishes of Charlbury, Shipton, Taynton and Widford – then in Gloucestershire – had rights of common within the forest for horses and horned cattle, except oxen. Leafield, Langley and Shorthampton enjoyed sheep pasturage on waste Crown lands inside the wall and one or two hamlets had similar grazing rights on private land, again within the wall. The keepers well knew the extent of these sheep walks and impounded any strays. No swine were allowed. The officers of the forest were: a ranger, a launder (keeper of forest lawns), four bailiffs (or keepers), two verderers and a woodward. The two verderers were chosen by the freeholders of the county and had no salary but each received a brace of bucks and a brace of does annually.

In 1809 Arthur Young made a report on the agriculture and forestry of Oxfordshire. He said there were no sizeable oaks in Wychwood and was chiefly concerned with the lawlessness of the place and strongly recommended enclosure. 'The morals of the whole surrounding country demand it imperiously,' he said. 'The vicinity is filled with poachers, deer-stalkers, thieves, and pilferers of every kind; offences of almost every description abound so much, that the offenders are a terror to all quiet and well-disposed persons; and Oxford gaol would be uninhabited were it not for this fertile source of crime.'

The stories of Tom, Dick and Harry and of the Swinbrook Highwaymen, as well as the Murdered Stranger, bear this out to a certain extent, though Arthur Young seems to underestimate the activities of the Chiltern Highwaymen and it must be remembered that it was to Gloucester that Tom and Harry were taken. Actually the forest was reprieved until 1862, and the riotous scenes of the forest fair probably played their part in bringing about its closure.

The memory of the Dunsdons – Tom, Dick and Harry – is one still fresh in tradition, though different aspects of it are remembered by different people. They came of a respectable yeoman family at Fulbrook. The cottage they lived in has been pulled down and its stones were taken to build a house at Minster Lovell which is named after them. This accounts for the tradition that the Dunsdons were born at Minster Lovell. The eldest of them, Richard, was born in 1745. The three brothers went to the bad and took to the forest, which in those days came down almost to Fulbrook. They had a little cottage at Icomb, which had an underground passage to a cave in a wood close to the road, where they stabled their horses and hid their treasure. Mr Andrews – whose oral recollections are given below – knew a man who lived in this cottage but the passage had then been filled in. They took their horses to a smith at Fifield to be shod. They left them outside the smithy at dead of night and called next night, leaving money in payment. The Bird in Hand at Capp's Lodge was their chief meeting place. This was a notorious tavern on the edge of the forest, resorted to by the wilder sparks among the gentry for cock-fighting. The tavern has gone, but the remains of the cock-pit can still be seen and not far from it, on Habbergallows Hill, stands the gibbet oak where the remains of the Dunsdons were hung.

The Dunsdons started with petty robberies – of farmers coming home from market and the like – but gradually grew bolder, until at length they robbed the Oxford to Gloucester coach of £500. This made them notorious. Later they laid a scheme to rob Tangley Manor. The squire was known to be on a journey, leaving his wife and children alone with the servants. The Dunsdons were overheard discussing the project at Capp's Lodge and the butler was warned. He called in the constables the night on which they were expected and they watched silently inside the front door. It was an old and heavy one, with a hole guarded by a movable wooden shutter through which visitors could be inspected. Towards midnight this shutter was pushed aside from without and a hand and arm were thrust through, groping for the great key. The butler slipped a rope round it and tied it firmly to the handle. There was a torrent of muttered oaths from the outside and then a voice saying: 'Cut! Cut!' There were smothered groans and the arm dropped into the house. The constables and the menservants unlocked the door and started in pursuit but nothing was to be seen except bloodstains leading away from the door.

Dick was never seen again, so it was presumed that it was he whose arm was amputated and that he had bled to death on the way home. However, Tom and Harry remained and continued their robberies until they were captured in 1784. Curiously enough it is the memory of the capture which remained vivid among the forest men, though the more picturesque tale of the midnight attack and the severed arm is remembered in Burford in 1971. Mr Andrews of Swinbrook recorded the tradition which he received of the capture:

This is about the Dunsdons. I'm going to try and tell you the story as I heard it from an old man who lived in Swinbrook many years ago. They were three highwaymen, Henry and Thomas, and a third brother – I don't know what his name was; he was supposed to have been shot at Swinbrook Vicarage while doing a burglary. One of their burglaries was at Tangley House on the way from Burford to Stow, down in the valley. I have seen the hole [in the door] that he put his hand through . . . They were Fulbrook men, lived there in a little cottage for quite a number of years, but they did most of their 'work' at the village of Icomb, and I have heard say there is a tunnel running from a little cottage at Icomb up to the Stow Road. It comes out into a little wood.

Henry and Thomas were at the gambling house at Capp's Lodge not far from Fulbrook, on one Capp's Lodge Fair day [they had one every year]. They were in the gambling house bragging about 'no-one wouldn't take them', and the landlord, in jest, being as he knew them, said, 'well' he says, 'I could take the pair of you myself' he says [that was Harry and Tom]. So he made an attempt, in jest, and one of them fired; he had a lot of coppers in his pocket and they reckon it glanced off them. They were arrested by the other men in the gambling house; they were taken to Gloucester and hung [Capp's Lodge in those days was in the county of Gloucestershire], brought back and gibbeted on the Fulbrook–Shipton road, on the right-hand side; the tree is still there. That is the story as I was told from the same old man who told me about Millin's Tree. This old man said his grandfather could remember when they were brought back from Gloucester in an ordinary farm cart and taken up to Capp's Lodge and put on the tree. That is the story as I had it, as a boy; whether correct I don't know, but I had it on good authority; I don't think he would have said so unless he was sure.

In the nineteenth century the reputation of Wychwood as the home of robbers continued to be as bad. In the 'Hungry Forties' many who might otherwise have been respectable became desperate and robbery was very common. It was so much dreaded that special precautions were taken against it. At the Crown Inn at Finstock, for instance, where there was the cupboard type of staircase, the top of the door was sawn off so that anyone on the landing above could see over it into the hall-way and take a pot-shot at a robber. One night the landlord, Mr Goodman, heard a clatter downstairs, picked up the fork used to put whin on the fire and ran into the bar in time to see a man with a blackened face climbing out of the window. He had knocked a steelyard weight into a tin tray.

The next day a man came into the village shop and the woman keeping it said: 'What a lot of black you have on your face!' So the identity of the robber became generally known, though he was not proceeded against.

Another man was less lucky. There was a robbery at College Farm, Chadlington. The thief got away with his spoil but left his hat behind him. In those days men wore the same hat for 20 years on end and it became characteristic. The lost hat was taken to Chipping Norton market and set upon a pole. Presently a Duns Tew man came along and said, 'That's so-and-so's hat from our place.'

'Ah, so it is,' said another – and so the robber was caught. He must have ranged far afield, as the Dunsdons did, for the Tews are quite a distance from Chadlington.

These were petty thefts, but murder was not uncommon. John Kibble, author of *Historical and Other Notes on Charlbury*, tells the story of one that happened in his grandfather's time. After one

Charlbury New Year's Fair, a dealer who had stopped the night at the Crown Inn at Finstock set off to ride to his home. He had refreshed himself at the Bull Inn and there he had taken out his pocket book, which he hid before setting out in the pocket in the lining of his waistcoat. It had been seen, and before he got to the first milestone he was set on and murdered. The robbers could not find his wallet but took his hat, a low-crowned boxer, and by this they were recognised. The horse bolted and returned to the Crown at Finstock, where it also was recognised.

An even grimmer story was told at Leafield in 1962 by Mrs Falconer, then an old lady of more than 80. It had happened in her childhood. An unknown stranger had arrived by train at Shipton-under-Wychwood and had gone to the inn to find a guide through Wychwood to Witney. It was the eve of the annual fair at Leafield. Some young Leafield men were at the Shipton Inn and they noticed that the stranger was well-to-do, with a gold watch and plenty of money. They said that if he waited till the pub closed they would guide him through the forest. Next day Mrs Falconer's uncle, who was cutting brushwood in the forest, heard groans coming from a thicket near and found a stranger, terribly wounded and unable to speak. He was taken to the inn but because it was all cleaned out for the wake he was put into an outhouse where he died, unrecognised. He is buried in Leafield churchyard as an unknown man.

The police came from Oxford to try to discover the murderers but the secret was kept from them, though quite a number of people in the village knew it. An old ne'er-do-well in the village offered to tell Mrs Falconer's mother who it was that had the gold watch if she would give him a drink of beer. He had his beer, but he still refused to tell her. The family had some clue to the identity of the stranger, however, for one of Mrs Falconer's aunts was in service at Witney, where the family was expecting the arrival from Canada of a rich uncle, who never came or was heard of again. Their plausible conjecture was that he was the stranger, but the family was never told and the body was consigned to an unnamed grave. A similar tale told in Laurie Lee's *Cider with Rosie* of a hamlet near Stroud shows that Wychwood was not the only lawless place in the Cotswolds.

Gangs of sheep-stealers probably took refuge in Wychwood with other outlaws. There is a grim story told of Worsham Bottom, a reputedly haunted spot on the A40 road between Witney and Burford. I was investigating the story of Black Stockings, a spirit supposed to stop horses and pull their riders off their backs and I was told that this was a tale put about by highwaymen and that the true ghost of Worsham Bottom was that of a shrieking boy. He had seen the sheep-stealers at work and had been skinned alive by them: it is his ghost that runs shrieking along Worsham Bottom. I have not found confirmation of this grim tale but it points to a tradition of sheep-stealing more wild and desperate than that of the ordinary shepherd tempted by starvation to make away with one of his flock.

Poaching was another custom which increased lawlessness both among the people of the forest and the villages on its fringe. From the time of the Norman Conquest, if not earlier, poachers must have considered themselves within their rights and so long as the forest was inhabited by a mixed body of gipsies, squatters, fugitives and woodmen it would have been difficult to keep any control or record. Tenants of the manor of Charlbury had rights of felling and lopping and the burgesses of Burford claimed an annual day's hunt on Whit Monday until the reign of Queen Elizabeth, when this was commuted for the annual custom of sending a boy and girl up to Capp's Lodge, the keeper's house nearest to Burford, to fetch down a deer and hind to be hunted by the citizens of Burford. The Charlbury hamlets had grazing rights in the forest, as had Shipton-under-Wychwood on the other side. These long-held rights would account for the comparative respectability of poaching in the eyes of the local inhabitants, in spite of rigorous laws passed against it. In 1303 even Edmund Langley, the chief verderer, was accused of poaching. In 1662 a statute under Charles II empowered Richard Legge, the chief ranger, to take away all setting dogs, guns, etc. within ten miles' compass and till the end of the nineteenth century the keepers had a right to search all the cottages for hidden venison.

Many nineteenth-century poaching anecdotes are preserved by tradition in the forest villages and some are given by Muriel Groves in her *History of Shipton-under-Wychwood*, a book compiled from the researches of the Shipton Women's Institute. There was much boasting of poaching exploits and of notable dogs. These were mainly of the lurcher type and could run down deer or drive them into nets. One old man used to brag of being caught in a net with the deer. A deer was driven into the net and he crept in to kill it but a second deer dashed in after him and the two deer and the man were tangled up in the net together. Somehow he managed to kill both deer but they were too heavy for him and his mate to carry home. They took one between them, hid the other in the fern and fetched it home next night.

There were different methods of killing the deer. Sometimes pointed stakes were hammered in at their customary jumping places, so that the deer impaled themselves on them; sometimes a piece of the forest wall would be knocked down and the deer driven out to be shot down at leisure. On occasion parties were bold enough to go netting within the forest walls. When the deer was safely caught the next problem was to hide them until they could be sold or eaten. There were various hiding places. The most famous perhaps was the altar tomb in Burford churchyard, whose top lifted to make a snug larder for a whole carcase. There was also said to be a hollow rick standing on the wold, the entrance to it hidden by a wattle hurdle. The leads on the church roofs made convenient hiding places and whole deer were often hauled up to be hidden behind the ornamental balustrade. As for taking game to market, Walker the Shipton carrier had a false bottom to his cart in which he drove the venison to Oxford. Much was also sold in Burford for a few pence a pound and Witney provided a good market for Finstock and other hamlets.

Those who preferred eating it themselves—and it was rare indeed for the country people to taste any meat except what they poached—ran some risk of being discovered and that might well mean transportation. Mrs Groves gives two anecdotes of hidden pies in her book, one told her by her mother, who used as a child to stay with her grandmother at Milton. One day an old woman came running into the house with a large yellow pie in her hand and asked if she might put it down in the cellar. The little girl, rather puzzled, said she supposed she could. She told her grandmother about it but was hushed. It was not till some time later that she learned that the keepers were going round the cottages that day, searching for stolen venison. A more picturesque story is of a woman who had a large pie in her hands when the keeper came to the door. It was too late to look for any hiding place, so she put her baby on the pie and spread its wide skirts above it. Her prompt action saved her husband from transportation.

Some of the poaching stories were told with a good deal of amusement. 'Meetinger John's Shot' was a popular one. A Shipton man who worked at one of the farms on the edge of the forest noticed a fine deer browsing among the undergrowth one evening. It was there next day and he reported it to the poaching gang, who had many of the respectable tradesmen among their numbers. They confirmed the report, picked out 'Meetinger John' as the marksman and set up a kind of rough ladder so that he could shoot over the wall. The beast was there again in the dusk. He fired and a terrible braying broke out – he had shot an old donkey belonging to one of the Wychwood gipsies. Next day an old gipsy granny came round to tell of her loss and the poaching gang made up a handsome collection to pay for it.

The Milton quarrymen were amongst the most efficient of the poachers and they tolerated no encroachment of strangers. In the 'Hungry Forties' bands of men came down from the Black Country, poaching and purloining. The forest keepers appealed to the Milton quarrymen, who turned out in strength to help them. Their leader was a notorious poacher, Jack Smith, who took a flail as his weapon. With this he had the misfortune to kill one of the marauders, but at his trial he showed his billycock hat shorn in two by his opponent's stick and the jury brought in a verdict of justifiable homicide.

Even more tragic tales than this are told. One of the most notable is that of 'Millin's Oak'. Mr Andrews made a recording of the Swinbrook version of the tale in 1971.

Now, I'm going to start first of all at Hit or Miss, the public house just at the top. That was a public house, and the tree is in Hensgrove Wood, the common in those days which should still be a common, but the Forestry have taken over and have planted trees. There had used to be a high wall, quite six to seven foot high, which was before my time, that I've been told from an older man, and the deer were enclosed in there where the men of Swinbrook and all around the area used to go poaching the deer by night. Well, John Millin, the keeper, was out one night, and he was shot at the tree. A man shot him. Where he came from was either Leafield or Fordwells. Thinking it was a deer, he went up to the tree, and found it was the keeper, and made off. Two men of Swinbrook were poaching at the same time, but not with him, and they walked up, found the keeper, picked him up, and brought him back to Swinbrook Hit or Miss. So he was taken there, they were arrested, tried for the murder, and hung, Pittaway and James of Swinbrook. Well, when the old man at Leafield was laying at his last he confessed that it wasn't Pittaway and James of Swinbrook that shot Millin, he says, It was I, but, he

says, I didn't know it was Millin at the time, he says, I saw a
movement at the oak tree and I shot, he said, but when I found
it was the keeper I made off.

Well now, that was the history to the Millin's Tree, and the
name a few years ago was quite plainly written, ' J.M. ', on the
tree, but whether it is still there now, I don't know. But I know
where the tree is. It's about on the Fordwells road where you come
to the two gates. One goes through a little piece of the common,
straight through into Hensgrove Wood, and another gate opposite
it goes into Stockley Wood, and if you go just in through the
common, and take a right-hand incline, the first big oak-tree is
Millin's Tree.

Millin's Oak, which stood in Hensgrove, has now been cut down.
The Hit or Miss was the house just above that in which Mr Andrews
now lives. It used to have a sign showing a poacher shooting at a
pheasant. This inn, as well as the Bird in the Hand, shows how much
poaching was accepted as a way of life. In those days there was a
wide strip of common land on each side of the Swinbrook to Fordwells road, where people could graze their sheep and children could
play. They used to climb up on the high wall round the grove and
watch the deer. The Swinbrook sheep wore bells when grazing on
the common. Before Lord Redesdale sold the land to Mr McKinnon
he took down the high wall (by then in very bad repair) and rebuilt
it into the lower wall alongside the Fordwells road, thus enclosing
the common, which has now been taken over by the Forestry
Commission.

A sidelight is thrown on this story in Kibble's book on Charlbury. He used to lodge with an old woman who had as a girl
brought evidence which was accepted as proof against James and
Pittaway.

She had seen them set out on their poaching expedition and not
till the deathbed confession of the killer did she realise that they
were innocent. She was said to suffer much remorse for it, but that
of the guilty man must have been much greater. He is stated in Mrs
Groves' *History of Shipton-under-Wychwood* to have come from the
Shipton district but this is a vague ascription, as many of the forest
hamlets were in Shipton parish. An old lady from Shipton is said to
have walked in her pattens all the way to Oxford to hold an interview with the accused men before their execution. It is possible that
she had some suspicion of the real culprit. These various traditions

are worth collecting, for they make a valuable contribution to social history.

In a district as isolated as Wychwood and its villages and inhabited by people so primitive it is inevitable that many supernatural beliefs and traditions should be perpetuated. Ghost stories were particularly common and only a selection of these can be given. Tape recordings from Mrs Claridge of Finstock, Mrs Falconer of Leafield and Mr Andrews of Swinbrook may be of interest as hitherto unpublished material.

Mrs Claridge's recording was taken in 1968. The first is slight but interesting as recording a folk method of laying a ghost, which in this case took the form of a black dog, though probably supposed to be informed by a human spirit.

This is Eileen Claridge talking of ghosts which are supposed to have happened at Wilcote Woods. At one time of day they got a newly-born baby and clappers and a priest and there was two small ponds, and they said a prayer over the baby, they threw one clapper into one pond and one into another to lay a big black dog, and if all these should return together, they say the ghost will re-appear.

The second is also an animal spirit and the third is something in the nature of a poltergeist manifestation, though it may be related to the fourth, for the maid may have formerly occupied the room in which Mrs Claridge slept.

Now this is my own experience of a ghost. When I was cycling to Finstock just above Finstock Halt I saw a huge nanny-goat dragging a chain. I cycled fast to try and catch the nanny-goat. On meeting my young man, which is now my husband, I said to him, Did you see that nanny-goat, and he said he didn't, and it disappeared down the old Coach road. On the previous Sunday a woman from Stonesfield saw exactly the same nanny-goat, and it disappeared down the Coach road but I have never known what was the results of this nanny-goat.

On another occasion when I was working at Finstock as housemaid, I was in the bedroom and in the bed and I was awakened by a noise like an aeroplane coming over me, and all of a sudden all the clothes was lifted off of me and thrown back onto the floor. I lit the lamp to see what had happened, and there was nothing there, but after that I never slept in that bedroom without I had a lamp going.

On another occasion at the same house before I went there to work, a cook went off with the young housemaid's young man and the young housemaid was so upset that she went and drowned herself in the lakes in Wychwood Forest. Her ghost was seen some long time after that by a man from Charlbury. I knew the man that saw her, and at the time when the man saw her she was still wearing her uniform. He thought it was a maid, but he discovered afterwards that it was her ghost. It was the ghost of the young lady that drowned herself in the Kennels Lakes. It was when I was working at Finstock House when I was seventeen, and I'm fifty-two now.

Mrs Falconer had a number of ghost stories, some personal reminiscences and some accounts of traditions. She was born and brought up at Kingstanding, a row of cottages within the forest, a piece of raised ground where the kings visiting the forest were said to have stood while the game was driven towards them. As a girl she had an experience of a ghostly coach. Traditions of these coaches were fairly common in Oxfordshire and the Cotswolds, but she claimed to have experienced this apparition herself.

She and her mother were glovemakers and indeed she continued to make gloves almost to the time of her death. It was the custom for the cut-out leather for the gloves to be distributed at the George Inn in Leafield and picked up by the gloviers, who brought back their finished goods and were paid accordingly – not very highly. Mrs Falconer and her mother had returned their patterns, picked up new ones and were returning through the forest to Kingstanding when they heard a great trampling and jangling behind them. The road was narrow and the verges steep there and they climbed up among the bushes to get out of the way. A coach and horses passed them at a gallop along the narrow road where coaches never went, failed to turn the corner, went straight over into the ditch and vanished. They never saw it again but they never forgot it.

It was just such another coach as old Mr Bayliss of Minster Lovell heard crossing the Shipton to Chipping Norton road at the Churchill turn and presumably such another as old Lady Tanfield used for riding over the roofs of Burford.

While still a girl Mrs Falconer went into service at Fairspeare, a house of some size on the outskirts of Leafield. There was a lane called Black Dog Lane which passed the back drive to the house. It was haunted by a black dog and the maids on their nights out would never wait for their young men in the lane but stood inside the gate for safety. Mrs Falconer was too young to go out, so she never saw the black dog, but one night she and the cook, looking out of the bedroom window which they shared, saw a man going to and fro from the house to the little well-house in the garden, wheeling a barrow. It was a bright moonlight night and they watched him for some time, thinking he was a thief, but were too timid to give the alarm. Next morning, however, they reported what they had seen to their master and he searched both the house and the well-house. A curious thing is that Fairspeare is still said to be haunted by a gardening ghost who turns on the watering taps and goes to and fro to the well-house.

Mrs Falconer's most interesting traditions, however, were those of witchcraft, for witchcraft beliefs were rampant in the forest. At one time they had an old woman living next door to them who was reputed to be a witch. Mrs Falconer talked to me several times about her and finally recorded a rather summary version of it. The old woman was the wife of a retired cattleman whose place was taken by Mrs Falconer's father. On one occasion there was a commotion among the cattle at night and, going out, he saw the old woman rising up from the ground in her nightgown with her white hair streaming and in a kind of singing voice she said to him, 'Never mind, John, you do your work and I'll do mine.' This anecdote is omitted from the taped account:

When I was a little girl my mother had a new baby, and of course I was in the bedroom when this old lady came up in the bedroom and was talking to my mother, and then the dog belonging to her began to howl. My mother was very concerned and she said, 'Oh, do make that dog stop his noise, I hate to hear a dog howl.' Then this old lady said: 'Let 'en 'owl. He's 'owling arfter that child.' And 'er said, 'Is anything the matter with the child?' 'No, not that I know, except that it's going to die.' And my mother was very concerned about it, and it did die, it died when it was height days old. And of course my mother was very concerned about it and main frightened, and she wouldn't let anybody go anywhere near for days for fear they'd tell her something to hurt this baby what was the matter. They went to Charlbury, which is ever so

G

far, about four or five miles, to fetch the doctor to see if there was anything the matter, and he said, 'No, there's nothing the matter with it. No earthly reason why it should die,' but it did die, and that's all I can tell you.

And some years after that, or some time after that, this old lady did die, and my mother went in to look after her from next door and she said, 'Rhoda, bring my purse off the table.' And my mother said, 'Why do you wants the purse for? You can't spend money. You aren't able to get up.' 'I wants my purse. You give it me. I can't open it. You open it for me and then I can manage.' My mother opened this purse and there was a quantity of sovereigns in it, my mother saw them quite plain, but she never counted them to know the quantity. And she says: 'Oh, that's all right. I shan't be here many more days.' She counted 'em up. 'My money'll last till then, and when that's gone,' she says, 'I shall go, because I'm not able to go to fetch any more.' And she did die, and when the daughter that belonged to this poor lady, the daughter, my mother said to her, 'You'd better take care of that purse, because,' she said, 'I don't like being here alone with that purse. Because,' she said, 'your mother had it to look at, there's a lot of money in it, you take care of it,' and the old lady said, 'Let it alone! Leave it there!' And so they never moved it, and the daughter and my mother was there when she died. And when she died and they'd done different things to her, like what they has to do, one of them saying, 'You'd better take care of that purse, and see that's safe,' they opened the purse, and there was nothink in it, it was quite empty. The devil had took her and the money together.

Mrs Falconer also lived next to an old woman who was believed to be a shape-shifting witch. Men used to see a hare running past and would then find the old woman at her cottage door, panting and out of breath. But Mrs Falconer said she was a quiet neighbour and friendly and she didn't credit the tale.

One of the most persistent hauntings recorded on the fringe of the forest was that of old Sir John Reade of Shipton Court. There was a tragic story attached to him. In the 1860s Sir John was a drunkard and his old butler, Sindon, seems to have been something of a crony. One day the two came rather drunk out of the inn and went up together to the drawing-room. After some time there was a crash and Sir John called for help. The footman, Wakefield, and others hurried to the room and found the butler lying impaled on one of the tall fire-dogs on the fender.

The story pieced together afterwards was that Sindon insisted on ringing for more drink and Sir John, saying that he was drunk enough already, threw the bell-pull over one of the pictures. Sindon climbed on a chair to pull it down and either fell or was pushed over. At any rate he died of his injuries and a verdict of accidental death was found at the inquest. Wakefield was one of the witnesses. Rumours of foul play began to spread through the village and the body was exhumed but the same verdict was found. From that day Sir John was a sober and remorse-haunted man. He depended greatly on the footman, Wakefield, raised first to the position of butler and afterwards promoted to the management of the estate. On Sir John Reade's death in 1868 he left the estate and his gold-headed cane to his 'faithful servant Joseph Wakefield' on condition that he take the name of Reade. The will was disputed but upheld and Wakefield succeeded, only to be generally ostracised.

After this, tales of haunting began to spread around. Mrs Groves collected some of these from oral sources 65 years later. One was from the niece of a footman at Shipton Court who was told it by her uncle. A new housemaid asked him a number of years after Sir John's death, who the old gentleman was who was staying in the house. She insisted that she had met him several times on the stairs. From her description it was evidently Sir John. Shortly after his death a little girl said to her grandmother: 'Grammer, I thought you said Sir John was dead.' 'So he is, my dear.' 'Well, Grammer,' the little girl said, 'I have just seen him outside the gates.' These stories received very wide currency, until one day a group of strange clergymen was seen walking about the village. They had come to consult about laying the ghost. They met at the Lamb Inn and finally laid him in the little stream that goes under the road near the railway station. After that the stories of haunting diminished, but Mr Andrews of Swinbrook recorded a haunting many years later when he and another man were working at Shipton Court. It took the form of a sudden and very strong wind that arose in the house when it was a calm day outside.

Mr Andrews also recorded a haunting at Swinbrook of the type that often appears in psychic journals:

There were two of us saw it, and I'm not telling you just where

it was because I don't want anybody to be nervous. I've never
seen it since, but I was told that the same thing was seen twenty
years before.

Another fellow and I were going along the road one night, talking together like it might be you and me now, when for some
reason we both suddenly stopped talking and came to a dead
halt. Then we saw in front of us something blocking the road;
it was jet black and about the height of a piano. Then it changed
into a column about the height and shape of a man, but seemed
to be made of smoke – moving smoke, sort of zig-zag. Then it
began to move; you know how a dog creeps sideways when it's
frightened? It reminded me of that somehow. It came a bit
towards us and a bit sideways, as if it wanted to get past. My mate
pulled out his torch and flashed it on, and I took it from him
and went over to where the thing was and searched, but there was
nothing, only old dead stinging-nettles by the roadside. 'Come
on,' said the other chap, 'there's nothing there,' and we went on;
but later we talked about it and we'd both seen the same thing,
and he said, ' I reckon it was a ghost.'

There was a little house close by there, and the old lady living
in it asked me to go and examine the walls and wall-paper in her
bedroom, to see if anything was loose, because she said she heard
such peculiar noises in the night. I went all over that paper but
there was nothing whatever wrong with it. Another time I was
calling there, and there was a woman ill in bed in that room
upstairs, and when somebody went in to see her she said 'What
a terrible rough day outside!' But it was a beautiful day, warm
and quiet and no wind at all.

Some of the Wychwood wells were considered holy in pre-
Christian days and have been resorted to until the recent closure of
the forest as a nature reserve. On Easter Monday the people of
Leafield considered it their right to go to one of the forest springs to
make ' Spanish water '. This was kept as a remedy for almost every
disorder. On Easter Monday I have met troops of Leafield people
going through the forest with their bottles to make Spanish water.
The forest hamlets, as the word implies, had no churches of their
own and their general burial place was at Shipton-under-Wychwood.
The coffins were carried through the forest by hand, accompanied

by a band of mourners. Sometimes this was a sober procession but it was often riotous and gave offence in later and more decorous times. As roads became available and churches sprang up the custom died out.

On one occasion the coffin was lost for several weeks. It was a very snowy day and as they struggled through the drifts one of the bearers saw an untimely squirrel. They dropped the coffin and began to hunt it. The chase was a long one and when they came back the coffin was drifted over and could not be found. The funeral had to be postponed until the snow melted. These tales of lost coffins are in oral tradition over various parts of the country. In some of them the Devil removes the corpse.

The village feasts, originally held on the day of the patronal festival, were great occasions in the forest villages. That at Leafield, which lasted two days, was a particularly rowdy one. A kind of extension of these was the notorious forest fair which flourished in the nineteenth century.

The origin of this was peculiar – if the account given is true. The Earleys of Witney were a quiet Quaker family, who disliked the riot and bustle of Witney Feast. So towards the end of the eighteenth century Mr Earley invited a few friends to go with him to a picnic in Wychwood on the feast day. The treat was much enjoyed and next year some more friends asked to join them. The outing grew in popularity and by 1806 it was attended by 10,000 people. Stalls were set up for cloth, hosiery, flannels and hand-spun linen and many people did their annual shopping at Forest Fair. Witney Feast was held on the Feast of the Nativity of the Blessed Virgin (8 September) and the Forest Fair was on the Wednesday after that. The fair continued to grow, excursion trains were run and in the 1850s many thousands attended it. The Duke of Marlborough stopped the fair in 1856 and in 1862 the forest lands were enclosed and many people lost the little extra gains that made their living tolerable: grazing rights for their beasts, kindling and firewood, brushwood for hurdles, wild birds' eggs and wild fruits – to say nothing of the game that they could pick up by the way. Many were moved out of the forest and resettled in Leafield, Burford and Charlbury. Their descendants have become prosperous labourers or small tradesmen but still the Wychwood Forest blood is in their veins and the old traditions linger.

7 Rogues and Highwaymen

ONE OF THE MOST INTERESTING EXHIBITS in the small folk museum in Filkins kept by George Swinford, the retired stonemason, is a highwayman's horse-shoe. Everyone will remember how Robert the Bruce, after killing Red Comyn before the high altar in Dumfermline, made his escape by turning the shoes on his horse's hoofs so that the tracks seemed to lead in the opposite direction. This would be death to a horse's hoofs, and Cotswold highwaymen knew a trick worth two of this – they shod their horses with circular shoes. The last chapter told us a good deal about the violent men and robbers who found a hiding-place in Wychwood but there are many highwaymen legends all over the Cotswolds. They may not have been quite so wild as the Chilterns, whose warden was disabled from holding a seat in Parliament because it was judged that he would have to keep a constant watch over his unruly Hundreds, yet highwaymen legends crop up all over the

Cotswolds, though not all the criminals were local men. Mr Freeman
of Swinbrook is an example of this. The Fettiplaces of Swinbrook
were an ancient and wealthy family with connections all over the
Cotswold countryside:

> The Lacies, Tracies and Fettiplaces
> Own all the manors, parks and chases,

is the old saying, but in the eighteenth century the direct male line
died out and, though the daughter's children took the Fettiplace
name, the line did not continue. By 1806 the two old Miss Fettiplaces
found the manor too big for them, retired up to Fairspeare and let
the manor to a Mr Freeman from London, who came down with
quite a retinue of servants and entertained lavishly. At least so it was
at first, but later on people began to remark that the servants were
rather rough and uncouth in their manners and that anyone paying
morning calls would find the whole place drowsy.

About this time there began to be a number of highway robberies
on the London–Gloucester road – none however within ten miles of
Swinbrook. This went on for a year or more until a well-armed
coachman shot one of the robbers and when he was taken into
custody he was recognised as Mr Freeman's butler. The whole house-
hold was arrested and it was then discovered that they were a
notorious London gang, who had made the Home Counties too hot
for them and had moved out west.

It was perhaps less of a surprise to the locals than to those a little
further afield. Mr Hill of Charlbury has collected a living tradition
from Mr Seckar, whose family in the eighteenth century were
inhabitants of Widford Manor, just upstream from Swinbrook. Mr
Seckar's grandfather was a stable boy at Swinbrook Manor in the
Freeman time and he was much puzzled because, however well-
groomed the horses were at night, they were always splashed and
bemired in the morning. The manor seemed to him a mysterious
place and he was never allowed to set foot in it. It is hard to restrain
a boy's curiosity, however, and one night after dark he managed to
make his way into the manor.

There was a long passage on the first floor with bedrooms opening out on each side of it. The boy heard a sound of shots upstairs
and stole up. All the doors were open along the passage and there
was a lighted candle in every room. Mr Freeman and the butler were

running along at top speed, shooting out every candle as they passed. The boy tiptoed out again, glad to escape with his life, but when Freeman and the butler were hanged at Gloucester he managed to get hold of the pistols – his grandson has them still. Young Seckar was lucky to get away unobserved.

I have already referred to the tradition of Worsham Bottom, or 'Ousen Bottom' as it is sometimes called, and there is a similar horrible tale at Bruern. The tale is parallel to that of the Dunsdons' attack on Tangley Manor. The family at Bruern were away, leaving the servants in charge, and a powerful band of sheep-stealers planned to attack the abbey. Their plans were somehow overheard, however, and an anonymous warning was sent to the servants, who armed themselves, got in help and beat off the assailants with loss. The next night horrible screams were heard outside and the men-servants armed themselves and went out to the rescue. They beat off the gang – but too late. They had been skinning the Bruern shepherd alive. Only his head was left whole. He was able to tell them before he died that the sheep-stealers believed he had given the warning and were avenging themselves. The Dunsdons were less cruel but even they were ready to punish anyone who stood out against them. Among Mr Kibble's miscellaneous notes there is a further anecdote about the attempt on Tangley:

Not long before the capture and the execution of the brothers Dunsdon, highwaymen, who were gibbeted at Capp's Lodge, there is a story told of an attempt of these desperate men, that failed.

On the night when they attempted to break into Tangley House by cutting a hole, yet to be seen, in the door, through which one of them, it is said, thrust his arm, when it was held and securely fastened inside, so he could not withdraw it. To get him away his mates cut his arm off, and as he disappears and does not figure in further exploits, he is thought to have died through bad surgery. In the house that night was a labourer from Milton-under-Wychwood, who was working at Chalk's Barn, threshing corn. He fired a gun, or a blunderbuss, from an upper window at the departing robbers, and they got to know who did this, but did not know him by sight. The Dunsdons shortly after went in search of him, their motto being 'an eye for an eye, a tooth for a tooth'. They waylaid him coming home from work, as he was going to Milton, but not knowing him, were not sure of their man. In the parley that took place he pretended that they were on the wrong track, that the man they wanted was yet at Chalk's Barn, and they at once set off to find him. As fast as ever he could travel he went for home, and was just got into his cottage when the men of vengeance arrived. They did not however do anything, but went off, and our hero was afraid to go to Tangley to thresh again till it so happened they were arrested, as is well known, and presently were swinging in the breeze from the gibbet tree to be seen at Capp's Lodge.

There are highwaymen traditions all over the Cotswolds, very often indicated by the names of the places where they were gibbeted, such as Tom Long's Post on Minchinhampton Common and possibly Stump's Cross, or such dubious tales as that of the inn which formerly stood at Ready Token off the Akeman Street road, whose landlord robbed and murdered travellers – confirmed, according to legend, by an excavation of the almost forgotten site, when skeletons and a few golden guineas were discovered. A stranger and more inexplicable story, however, and one in which fact and fiction are curiously entangled, is that problem crime generally known as 'The Campden Wonder'. The proved facts can be shortly enough stated. On 16 August 1660 William Harrison, the steward to the Viscountess Campden of Chipping Campden, set out to collect some rents due to his lady and did not return that night when he was expected. His wife, growing anxious, sent out John Perry, his servant, to look for him. He seems to have wandered about rather vaguely, meeting and speaking to one or two people, who afterwards confirmed his account of their conversations, but he returned in the morning, saying that he could not find his master.

In the meantime Mr Harrison's hat, neckband and comb were found in a furze bush near Ebrington by a woman who had been out gleaning. This made people suspect that he had been set on and robbed, but though great search was made there was no sign of his body. At this John Perry was arrested under suspicion of having robbed him. His story, such as it was, was confirmed by witnesses but he was held in custody for further questioning. He then began to produce a variety of stories, saying first that his master had been murdered by a tinker and then to others that the murderer was a gentleman's servant who hid the body in a bean-rick, which was searched but nothing was found. Presently his fancy took another turn and he said that if he was brought before a justice again he would confess the real truth.

Accordingly he was brought before the justice on 24 August and said that his mother and brother had murdered Mr Harrison but that he had had no part in it, except for informing them when money would be available, both on an earlier occasion when the house had been robbed of £140 and on this, when Mr Harrison was waylaid and murdered. The justice seems to have been rather sceptical for he warned John Perry that he might draw down innocent blood on his own head if his accusation caused the death of his mother and brother. This only made Perry more detailed and positive in his statements, in the course of which he implicated himself as an accomplice both before and after the crime.

Accordingly Joan and Richard Perry were arrested, both vehemently protesting their innocence. They were brought before Sir Christopher Turner at the September assizes on the two counts of robbery in 1659 and murder in 1660. They pleaded the benefit of the late Act of Indemnity for the robbery but again protested their innocence of the murder. Since no body had been found the judge dismissed the case. However at the next assizes they were brought before Sir Robert Hyde who so directed the jury that they were pronounced guilty and they were all three hanged on Broadway Hill. Richard and Joan were buried at the foot of the gallows but John's body was gibbeted. At the end even John protested that he knew nothing of William Harrison's death, who would return in seven years. The case was the blacker against Joan Perry because she was believed to be a witch.

In 1662 Perry's prediction was proved right, for William Harrison returned with a wild story of having been attacked and wounded by an unknown horseman, carried off to Deal and sold into slavery in Algiers. Mr Harrison was at this time a man of 70 and it seems doubtful if he would have survived all the hardships which he describes.

A careful and circumstantial account of the whole matter was given by Sir Thomas Overbury of Bourton-on-the-Hill, a grandson of that unfortunate Sir Thomas Overbury who was poisoned in the Tower at the instance of the Countess of Essex. It was published by Dr Thomas Shirley in 1676. Mr Harrison's open letter to Sir Thomas Overbury was published in it.

A careful assessment of the whole matter called *The Campden Wonder* was edited by Sir George Clark in 1959. The most probable explanation of Harrison's disappearance is to be found in the Notes by Lord Maugham in pages 80–98 of *The Campden Wonder.*

He suggests that Harrison had been embezzling his employer's money during the chaotic times of the Interregnum and, fearing that the re-establishment of law would bring his dishonesty to light, staged a mock murder and disappearance with the connivance of John Perry. The time of his disappearance was earlier than the Proclamation of Idemnity. The money supposed to be stolen earlier was probably in his hands and with this and his defalcations in 1660 he continued to live for two years and turned up at the end of it with a faked tale of kidnapping to account for his absence.

Probability is lent to this hypothesis by the fact that there was in existence the story of a man being sold to the Turks, taken as a slave by a Moorish doctor and being finally given a silver bowl by his master to secure his passage home – all motifs which feature in William Harrison's account. It was also said by Anthony Wood that after his return his wife fell into a depression and committed suicide. She might well be horrified by her husband's callousness in leaving innocent people to be put to death because of his absence. If that was so no one seems to have brought it home to him. His son had taken his place as agent, but he continued in good repute and was on the governing board of the school until his last illness.

It may be said that this strange disappearance is a well-authenticated piece of history and has no place among folk traditions but the novello produced by Mr Harrison to account for his absence and the strange witch stories which grew out of the general bewilderment made this actual happening a source of folk tradition.

As well as professional highwaymen and dangerous gangs of sheep-stealers there were ordinary working men who yielded to temptation and sometimes suffered for it, though a local conspiracy of silence often shielded them – as we found in Mrs Falconer's story of the murder of the stranger in Chapter 6. Poaching was condoned by village morality but there seems to have been less sympathy with sheep-stealing. The legend of Hangman's Stone at Preston near Cirencester illustrates this. There are fairly wide-spread variants of the tale, one on the Blackdown Hills, one on the borders of Wales and one in Allendale.

A sheep-stealer was carrying away a live sheep. His method was to tie the four legs together and sling the sheep over his shoulders. It was very heavy and when he came to the ancient Roman milestone at Preston he sat on it to rest himself. The sheep struggled, slipped off the stone and strangled him. Rudder suggests that this stone was a place of execution in Roman times and that the tale was invented to account for the name. In other versions the sheep-stealer heard a woodpigeon calling ' Take two, Davie ' and carried off two sheep accordingly. This adds a touch of grim comedy to the tale.

Vagabonds and sturdy beggars would be brought before the local justice and given summary punishment or dismissed. Most villages would have stocks to deal with this type of offender and some are still to be seen, such as those at Northleach. The ordinary villager who was drunk and disorderly would receive the same kind of treatment. Mr George Swinford, part of whose folk museum at Filkins is in the old lock-up, can tell us something of the traditional procedure.

The lock-up is a long narrow cell with a stone bench at the back, whose only comfort would have been a litter of straw, probably not always very fresh or dry. It was lit and ventilated only by holes bored in the strong oak door. A man convicted of drunkenness and rioting would be locked up for the night to be marched over to Burford to the justice in the morning. At the first light a devoted wife would get up, take some bread and cheese and buy half a pint of beer from the Lamb Inn over the road. At the same time she would borrow the landlady's tea-pot, into which she would put the beer. She would poke the spout through one of the holes, call to her husband inside and gently pour the beer into his mouth. Then she would push small pieces of bread and cheese through the biggest of the holes, so that her husband, with food and drink inside him, could face the four-mile trudge to Burford and the stern admonishments of the justice with a good heart. This is one of the many ways in which the Cotswold peasants managed to mitigate the hardships of their lot.

8 Birth, Death and Marriage

TWO THINGS ARE CERTAIN about every man alive in this world:
that he has been born and that he will die. Marriage is a matter of
choice and chance but the way in and the way out are inescapable.
They are also mysterious and for this reason are surrounded by many
beliefs and ceremonies. Many hundreds of years of belief in
astrology have made the date of birth important, though astrology
has sunk from an elaborate science founded on insufficient premises
to a superstition in which importance is given only to zodiacal signs.
The ephemerides, place and time of birth, planetary aspects and so
on are ignored – in popular belief that is – although there are still
people who claim astrology as a science and study it assiduously.
On the whole, however, the zodiacal superstition is sustained by the
popular Press, and thousands of people look eagerly at their daily
fortune with a half-playful interest and are glad to wear their lucky
month-stone. It is not common, however, for parents to be much

depressed to find their children born under Scorpio or Cancer.

In the same way the day-fatality rhyme, though often quoted is not taken seriously. In earlier times they had more importance. Certain qualities, among them immunity from witchcraft and power to perceive spirits, were ascribed to children born on Sunday and a 'chime-child' could see ghosts and was a natural healer.

What constituted a chime-child was understood differently in different parts of the country. In East Anglia a chime-child was one born in the chime hours, at 8, 10 or 12 but in Somerset, as Ruth Tongue was informed from her childhood, a chime-child was born between 12 and 1 on a Friday.

Ruth Tongue seems to have found some trace of this belief in the Cotswolds in a tale told her in 1925 by a Stroud resident at a picnic on Painswick Beacon. According to this tale Friday was considered an unlucky day to be born, as the birthday of those destined to be hanged or murdered. So when a Painswick woman had a baby at 12 o'clock on Good Friday night she called her Mary and got the priest to christen her at once to keep her safe.

The Painswick people, however, made nothing of that. The child was born on the unluckiest day of the year and was bound to come to a bad end. So she had a lonely childhood and went into the fields and woods where she taught herself a great deal about the virtues of herbs. When she grew up she had become a great healer of animals and stock, so that she was well known and eagerly greeted all over Oxfordshire and Gloucestershire; but in Painswick they still considered her a witch and when she went into a nearby haunted wood to fetch out a baby who had strayed into it and been lost, they thought worse of her than ever. Even the child's mother thought that she was a thief and a kidnapper. However, a young squire succeeded to the manor of Painswick and the people thought he ought to be warned, so they told him there was a Friday-born witch in the town. When the Squire knew they were talking of Mary, who had set his own hound's broken leg as good as new and was known for her healing touch at every market in the Cotswolds, he told them, straight out and angry, that they ought to thank God that they'd got a healer among them, a chime-child, born on a Good Friday at midnight. 'So,' he said 'I'll set the next fool in the stocks that doesn't treat our famous Wise Woman with care and courtesy.' After that they were all civil to Mary but Painswick folks are stubborn and there's no knowing what they thought.

If they thought little of it they seem to have forgotten it since, for I have not succeeded in finding any local trace of the tale. It is possible that it was a solitary invention or was founded on a Stroud legend, for Stroud and Painswick people have a traditional enmity. There seems no notion in Painswick that Friday is an unlucky birthday, nor have I been able to identify the haunted wood. In 45 years much can be forgotten and a tale told by a single narrator leaves scope for importation. I should hesitate to rate the Friday chime-child as a Cotswold belief on the foundation of this single tale.

Christening is still a matter of traditional as well as of religious importance, though there seem to be no traces in the Cotswolds – so far as I have been able to find – of the precautions formerly taken to preserve unchristened children from fairies or witches: the father's trousers laid across the cradle, the open scissors hung above it or crossed pins in the baby's clothes. We find a trace of the holiness of the newly christened child in the laying of the Wilcote black dog ghost which was mentioned in Chapter 6. In the *Annual Report of the Oxfordshire and District Folklore Society* for 1950 we find a short note on baptisms:

> Many local families have christening robes which have been handed down for generations, and which are always used when a new baby is baptised. It is still the custom for everyone who goes to see a new baby to place a silver coin in its hand. This is done by those who are not very intimate with the family as well as by close friends and relatives. There is an old belief that if a mother crosses the road before she has been churched after birth, really serious bad luck is bound to follow.

The giving of silver is still practised by elderly people when they pay a first visit to the baby. It is now rare for the family christening robes to be used, partly because of the large size of modern babies – particularly their heads – and partly because the fashion for the long robes has gone out. It is generally thought to be lucky for the baby to cry during the christening as a sign that the Devil is going out of him. The upper tier of the wedding-cake is still often kept to serve as a christening cake for the first baby. In the Cotswolds there is one record of the common tradition that the baby's first journey must be upwards but people do not now seem to think it unlucky to cut a baby's nails. So many babies are born in nursing homes now that many of the old birth customs such as the cutting of the ' groaning cheese' have disappeared.

The same is true of deaths. Many people nowadays die impersonal deaths in hospitals but in the 1950s the Oxfordshire and District Folklore Society recorded some well-rooted beliefs about death. Miss Bell of Kencot recorded a note about telling the bees of a death just below the Cotswold area, which holds good in the Cotswolds as well:

> When anyone dies in a house where bees are kept in the garden, the oldest occupant of the house must walk round each hive three times and repeat distinctly the name of the dead person three times. If this is not done for each hive separately the bees will desert. A man of Clifton Hampden omitted to do this when his daughter died in 1926 and all four hives of bees deserted.

The duty of watching beside the dead is still held to be important and candles are still lighted round the coffin. Mrs Groves of Shipton had some notes on the subject:

> As soon as a death has taken place, the windows should be flung wide open, so that the soul may escape. A dead person should never be left nor should a key ever be turned on him. You may leave the sick if you must, but you should never leave the dead. You should go out as little as possible while the corpse remains in the house.

No numbers must be used in measuring a corpse for its coffin according to Mrs Groves:

> A corpse should be measured for the coffin with a piece of string. You tie three knots in it, one for the length, one for the width at the shoulders and a third for the width at the hips.

No mention is made of the covering of the looking-glass immediately after a death – a precaution against the soul looking into it and being caught – nor have I found any Cotswold person who remembers that tradition. An old tradition which has, however, left its mark and is to be traced in every old churchyard would now be almost forgotten except for the tangible evidence that it has left behind. In examining the gravestones in every well-established churchyard one will find that the old ones are to the south of the church and the north side is filled up with later stones. This is evidence of the old belief that the north side of a church belonged to the Devil, the enemy of light and sun. Formerly only tramps and strangers and people suspected of suicide were buried on the north side of the church.

Marriage, as I said earlier, has not the inexorability of birth and death but it was felt to be ruled by Fate, and much divination, playful or serious, was practised by young people and particularly by girls to discover one's fate in matrimony. Most of these methods of divination were the same all over the country, as for instance, the Hallowe'en spells, roasting pairs of nuts together to see how they jump, peeling an apple in front of a mirror at midnight, filling one's mouth with water and running round the house, when the first man's name heard will be that of one's future husband. Or there was the well-known but sinister spell of sowing hempseed that belonged to Midsummer Eve, or the meal set out for sweethearts in ritual silence, or the induced divinatory dream, of which the simplest and most universal is to put a piece of wedding-cake under one's pillow. A peculiarly Cotswold piece of divination is that mentioned in Chapter 1 when girls went one by one up to the Whispering Knights at Rollright to hear what name the stones would whisper.

An unusual superstition had to do with St Valentine's Day. It was said that if a dark man crossed the threshold on 14 February an unmarried girl in the house would marry him before the year was out. A variation of the garter spell was used by North Hanborough girls in divining for a husband. A girl pinned her garters to the wall over her bed and placed her shoes beside it in the form of a letter 'T'. She got into bed backwards and said:

> I pin my garters to the wall
> And put my shoes in the shape of a T
> In hopes my true love for to see,
> Not in his apparel nor in his array
> But in the clothes he wears every day.
> If I am his bride to be,
> If I am his clothes to wear,
> If I am his children to bear,
> I hope he'll turn his face to me.
> But if I am not his bride to be,
> If I am not his clothes to wear,
> If I am not his children to bear,
> I hope he'll turn his back to me.

H

She had to remain silent for the rest of the night and her lover would appear in a dream, back or front as her fate ordained.

When we come to the wedding itself, fashions are always changing but many which are still in favour have deep roots. A white wedding is still popular, often with the veil which is thought to have its origin in the primitive oriental custom by which the bridegroom must not see the bride before the wedding. Until very recently it was thought unlucky for the bridegroom to see the bride on her wedding day before they met at the church. The riotous practical jokes still played on the newly wed couple are a survival of the horseplay at earlier weddings when there was no honeymoon and the bride was escorted by all the guests to her new home, where the whole party spent at least a night and often several days in horseplay and riot. All this used to be thought of as a contribution to fertility.

If a North Oxfordshire bride throws her bouquet out of a window after the ceremony, the bridesmaid who catches it, or is first to reach it, will be the first to marry; and similarly the girl who secures the first pin from the bride's dress when the latter is changing to go to her honeymoon will either be the next bride or will be lucky in some other way.

Lucky colours for marriage are still white and blue; green and yellow are unlucky. Gold is permissible, as the colour of light, and so is silver. The old rhyme is often quoted:

> Married in black, you'll wish you were back;
> Married in green, not fit to be seen;
> Married in brown, you'll never live in a town.

In Northleigh they say that a bride should never make her own dress, nor try it on entire before she sets out for the wedding. She should never look in a mirror with her veil on till the last moment.

It is very unlucky to lose or break a wedding ring. If the ring is dropped during the wedding ceremony, the one dropping it will be the first to die. The wedding ring ought not to be taken off.

In the choice of wedding days a Friday or any day in Lent is unlucky. Saturday, which is now the commonest day for weddings, used to be thought unlucky. June is the most fortunate month but from the time of the ancient Romans May was unlucky.

The bridal party must leave by the front door; so must the honeymoon couple. It is lucky to meet a sweep or for a black cat to cross the path but very unlucky to meet a funeral. It is a bad sign if a bride or bridegroom cuts a finger on the wedding morning. It is unlucky to call a bride by her maiden name after the wedding, or by her future name before it.

There are also a few local marriage omens. Two clocks striking together or two spoons together on a saucer portend marriage. A girl stumbling on the stairs will be married shortly but to look behind her breaks the omen. Some say the next person to come upstairs will be the one to marry.

From the point of view of the future husband, George Swinford quotes the Filkins description of what is desirable in a wife:

> She must be like and unlike three things. She must be like a snail to keep within her house; but she must not be like a snail to carry all she owns upon her back. She must be like an echo to speak when she is spoken to; but not like an echo to have always the last word. She must be like the town clock in regular habits and good time-keeping; but she must not be like it in speaking so loudly that the whole town can hear her.

When the marriage was over and the sober work of life was resumed there was as much possibility of unhappiness in earlier times as there is now, though there would be more attempts at adjustment and resignation. If a marriage was notoriously unhappy the indignation of the community would be roused against the one felt to be guilty in the partnership. This feeling would generally find expression in some form of ' rough music '. If the wife was supposed to be a scold or husband-beater her effigy would be carried in procession or acted in pantomime but in later days the demonstration seems to have been most commonly made against the man. In Gloucestershire a wife-beater would sometimes have loose straw laid outside his door to signify ' threshing done here ' but more commonly the demonstration would be a procession, with rhymes, songs and lampoons accompanied by every noise that could be made with pots, kettles, pans and rattles. This racket generally drove the offender out of the town.

A typical song directed against a wife-beater was given from South Stoke:

There is a man in our town who often beats his wife;
And any man who beats his wife deserves to lose his life,

So if he does it any more
We'll pull his nose right out before.

Holler boys, holler boys,
Make the bells ring.
Holler boys, holler boys,
God Save the King.

In Coombe they made rough music as late as the 1930s. It was directed at a woman accused of immorality. A young reporter set out to make a story out of it and asked the first woman he met. It happened to be the woman herself and she sent him away with a flea in his ear.

The last demonstration of rough music in Burford was directed against another type of marital misdemeanour. Legal divorce was a financial impossibility to the poor of England but a belief sprang up among them – and was even sometimes condoned by the clergy – that a man could legally part from his wife if he put a halter round her and exposed her for sale in the common market. This was sometimes an arrangement with a lover and quite amicably carried out, ending with a drink at an inn for all three parties and the two witnesses, but sometimes a husband would sell his wife to a stranger. The preliminaries to the Burford affair are not exactly known but in 1855 a Burford man sold his wife at Chipping Norton market for £25 – a very handsome sum, for half a crown was all that custom demanded.

The man who bought her lived at Simon Wisdom's cottages at the bottom of the town, down by the bridge. The town evidently no longer considered this a respectable way of arranging a divorce, so for three nights running they gave him rough music, with horns, trumpets, tin whistles and cans beaten with sticks. On the third night they burnt the man in effigy outside his door. This was too much for the sufferer. He burst out of the house with a pitch-fork, flung the flaming straw figure into the river and thrust a good many of the crowd in too. Mr Hambidge, who was a boy at the time, splashed through the river and escaped. In spite of this spirited demonstration the man felt that he could bear no more and gave the husband £15 to take back his wife again. Mr Hambidge told his daughter what he had seen but would never mention names, for he said that some descendants of the people were still living.

A more decorous but equally venomous attack was described to me on 2 August 1973 by Mrs Rogers, an old lady who had been born and had lived all her life in Painswick. It was directed against two maiden ladies the Misses Mason of Beacon House, the daughters of a doctor who had been much beloved and had lived to a great old age in the town. The daughters apparently became autocratic and meddlesome as they grew older and a torchlight procession was staged against them. Their effigies were borne through the town and at last burned, presumably on Beacon Hill. The Misses Mason behaved with great courage and dignity. They walked quietly up and down the street looking at the procession, apparently quite unconcerned, and no one molested them. This seems like a demonstration not against a marital offence but the offence of celibacy.

9 Plants, Trees and Animals

MANY SIMILAR BELIEFS about plants, trees and animals are held in all parts of Britain; some are peculiar to the North of England and Scotland and some are more prevalent in the West. A few are specially recorded in the Cotswold area, though not as a rule peculiar to it. Some of these have been noted by the Oxfordshire Folklore Society.

Flowers blooming out of season are very unlucky and a fruit tree blossoming twice in one year is a death omen. This is particularly so with apple trees, which have a strong magical significance. A single spray of apple bloom flowering among the ripe apples is thought to portend the death of one of the family. To pick up dead flowers found on the road is to pick up sickness. It is also unlucky to transplant flowers from the garden of a ruined house. White flowers, especially those with drooping heads such as snowdrops, are death omens. White may brought into the house is dangerous except on

May Day itself and in Oxfordshire white lilac is also avoided. Cuckoo flowers and poppies are equally unfortunate if brought into the house and in most parts of England cuckoo flowers are scrupulously left out of May garlands; curiously enough they are usually part of the garlands carried about by the Oxfordshire children. In Heyford it is said that if you look steadfastly into the heart of a poppy you will go blind.

Of the herbs, sage, rosemary and lavender are all essentially feminine plants and where they flourish it is a sign that 'the mistress is master'. A man in Charlbury is said to have chopped down a too vigorous sage bush in his garden some years before 1959, for fear his neighbours should think his wife ruled the house.

Clary, or wild sage, is locally supposed to be a legacy of the Roman occupation of Britain. The soldiers dropped the seed as they marched across the country. In proof of this, country people will point to the fact that it frequently flourishes along the old Roman roads. The same thing is said all over the country about nettles, supposed to have been imported by the Romans to brew nettle beer. St John's wort, in the Cotswolds as elsewhere, is a *fuga daemonis*: where it is worn or carried the Devil and witches have no power.

There are many traditions about planting vegetables. In the Cotswolds as elsewhere root crops must be planted in a waning moon and top crops in a waxing one. Parsley is a particularly tricky plant. It is dangerous to transplant it and fatal to be given a plant as a gift. A slightly safer way is for the owner to indicate a bed of parsley silently and for the recipient to come and dig it up in pretended secrecy. It is safer to sow it and this is a slow process, for it goes down to Hell three times – some say as many as nine – before it sprouts. It is said to grow best if sown with curses and better for a bad man than a good one but all is made safe if it is sown on Good Friday after coming back from church. The same date is good for potatoes. There are contradictory attributes given to parsley: by some people it is considered a fertility plant and by some sterilising.

Special dates are appropriate for planting. In Filkins they say that if you want a good crop of kidney beans you must plant them on Stow Market Day, that is 12 May and spring cabbages should be planted on Lechlade Fair Day (9 September).

Of the flowering and berry-bearing trees and shrubs holly, may and elder have the strongest folk significance in the Cotswolds. Holly, an evergreen and with bright red berries, had been a sacred tree from pre-Christian times. It has been christianised but there are probably some reservations about it. In Oxfordshire they say that holly for Christmas decorating must not be brought into the house – or presumably the church – before Christmas Eve, or left up after 6th January. In other parts of the country it is allowed to remain up until Candlemas. If this taboo is not observed you will have the Devil in the house. To burn green holly causes a death in the family. Holly cures chilblains, but rather drastically. They must be beaten with a holly bush till they bleed and the chilled blood is let out. In old days a bush of holly was hung up outside a house to indicate that wine was to be had there. It was the rustic sign of an inn, but a man jovially inclined would hang it up to invite his friends to join him. Holly was a symbol of masculinity as ivy was feminine.

Mistletoe was a plant with strong pagan associations and as such was never brought into the church. The single exception to this seems to have been in York Minster, where it retained its ancient function of being a plant of revelation and pardon and was laid on the altar through the Twelve Days of Christmas. In Herefordshire mistletoe was not allowed in the house until New Year's morning, in the middle of the Twelve Days of Christmas, but in the Cotswolds the more usual custom was observed and a kissing branch of mistletoe was hung up in a prominent place. It was considered suitable to kiss under the mistletoe when there was a berry and sometimes a young man who had won a kiss would remove a berry, so that in time the bunch would be stripped. This refinement of the custom is not now observed.

Holly, ivy and mistletoe are the winter shrubs; the hawthorn is immediately thought of as belonging to spring and the same relationship with life and death is to be observed in the beliefs about the hawthorn as one finds with the holly. Like the holly, the hawthorn has its season of beneficence. It is on May Day that the dew from the hawthorn tree beautifies a maid for ever, and 'a sprout well-budded out' is an auspicious gift. Flowering may brought into the house at any other time was supposed to bring illness and possibly death with it.

The elder may perhaps be thought of as the midsummer tree, and it too is ambivalent, though it is perhaps more malign than helpful. In the Cotswolds particularly the elder used to be thought of as the witches' tree. Just as all hares are not witches, but a flavour of witchcraft hangs over them because it is the favourite form for a witch to assume, so all elder trees are not witches but all elder trees are suspect. It was believed that an elder which was a transformed witch would bleed if cut. Elder wood was seldom or never burnt; people were often reluctant to cut elders and it was considered unlucky to use elder wood for making or mending furniture and particularly for making cradles. It is very doubtful if any of this is believed now, but most country people know about the belief. On the other hand the elder has its gentler side. Elder trees afford a shelter against flies and there is one belief that fairies can shelter from witches under elders. There is no fear of bringing elder flowers indoors; bunches of them are hung up to keep off flies. Elderflower and elderberry wine are both popular and are credited with curative qualities, as is elderflower tea.

Rose bushes, wild or cultivated, are midsummer flowers and are everywhere the symbols of true love. They were used in love spells, both for divination and for ensuring the return of an errant lover. A rose, and particularly a white rose, is also an emblem of secrecy and the wild brier is sometimes used to signify illicit love. So an illegitimate child is said to have been born 'under the rose'. In many of the great houses with plaster ceilings a rose is the central ornament. This was held to be a reminder that matters talked of at the table 'under the rose' must not be repeated outside that room. The white rose was the Jacobite symbol and the Jacobite glass at Chastleton is engraved with a design of roses. A white rose is thought to be particularly appropriate to plant over a virgin's grave and was often planted by a mourning lover. In many folksongs and ballads of tragic love a rose springs up spontaneously on the girl's grave and a wild brier on the man's and the two intertwine as a sign of their enduring love. In this motif the souls of the two lovers are embodied in the plants as Old Roger's was in the apple tree in the children's singing game.

Apple trees have always been significant and important. The custom of wassailing the apples on Twelfth Night was long followed in Gloucestershire and Worcestershire but naturally more in the apple-growing country (the Vale of Evesham and the Gloucester Plain) than on the Cotswolds. Apples were, of course, used in the Cotswolds as elsewhere for love divination and Hallowe'en sports. It has been suggested that the Hallowe'en ducking for apples is a survival of a method of allotting the lands for strip cultivation, such as is still employed at Yarnton in Oxfordshire, where each strip is represented by a marked ball.

Of the forest trees the oak is generally placed first. It was a sacred tree both in Celtic and in Scandinavian mythology, as well as belonging to Zeus and Jupiter. The village tree in most parts of the country was generally an oak, though it is interesting to notice that the village tree in Oxfordshire and the Cotswolds is often an elm. The oak was venerable for its longevity and for the lasting quality of its wood. It was everywhere sacred to the god of thunder and it was generally thought safe to shelter under it in a storm. The bobbins at the ends of blind cords are carved into acorns as a talis-man. It was a tree of many uses. The acorns provided food for swine and pigs – sacred animals – and its bark was used for tanning leather. It was a benevolent tree but it could also be formidable. Aubrey records in writing both of Wiltshire and Surrey that the oak was thought to scream when cut down :

> When an oak is felling, before it falls it gives a kind of shreikes or groanes, that may be heard a mile off, as if it were the genius of the oak lamenting. E. Wyld, Esq. hath heard it several times.

An oak coppice, where the oaks had been felled and shoots had sprung up from the stumps, was thought to be a sinister place after sunset.

The oak received a new publicity from Charles 11's refuge in the oak tree, afterwards celebrated on Oak-Apple Day or 'Shick-Shack Day' when school-boys wore oak apples in their button-holes and all who failed to do so were whipped with nettles. It had to be oak apples not acorns, for Oak-Apple Day was on 29 May, when no acorns would be ripe. Though many villages had elms rather than oaks as their central tree, there was likely to be an oak on the edge of a wood on the bounds of the parish, where the gospel would be read at the Rogation-tide procession and this would be called the Gospel Oak or the King's Oak. Where there was an extensive forest like Wychwood, which was extra-parochial, there would be a Gospel oak belonging to the forest, where, in pre-Reformation days, wandering friars would preach and sometimes marry the forest people and where royal proclamations would be made. The Duke's Oak in *A Midsummer Night's Dream* comes to mind as Shakes-peare's adaptation of the King's Oak. The withered remains of the Gospel Oak of Wychwood are still to be seen where the road bends towards Charlbury.

There was another King's Oak, a famous one in Woodstock Forest which was uprooted and chopped up by the Commonwealth

Commissioners when they came to take over the royal manor of
Woodstock in 1649. The wood was stored in the dining-room and it
was after this that the disturbances began which were described
in full by Robert Plot and in the pamphlet *The Just Devil of Woodstock*. If the whole affair was contrived by the Royalists it would
certainly gain credence among the country people as the protest of
the outraged sacred tree.

The ash in most parts of the country is as potent as the oak. Its
sacredness springs largely from Scandinavian mythology of the Ash
Ygg-Drasil which supported the foundations of the world and the
ash wood from which the gods made the first men. In the Cotswolds,
however, there seems little trace of Scandinavian tradition and here
the ash seems less important than in other parts of the country. The
well-known weather rhyme of the oak and the ash is often repeated,
however, and an ash-wood whipstock or goad is thought to be good
protection against witchcraft. Mrs Claridge, the wart-charmer, prefers a piece of ash wood to work with but I have not come across
the even-ash spell or any use of ash keys, nor any shrew ashes nor
a tradition of a split ash for the cure of rickets. Further research
might uncover these but it may well be that these charms, though
once used, have now sunk into oblivion.

Elms are looked on with some distrust because of their habit of
dropping a limb suddenly and of dying from the heart outwards.
Recently, of course, elm disease has caused a great number of elms
to be cut down. They are well-loved trees in the Cotswolds, however,
and are common around farms and in villages. One sowing precept
is to watch the elm leaves and when they are as big as a farthing,
plant your beans.

Pine trees are not very common in the Cotswolds. When a clump
of them is seen in a conspicuous place near a dwelling it is traditionally supposed that they were planted as a sign to fugitive Jacobites
that they could find safe harbour there. The pines were associated
with Scotland and the Stewarts.

Many folk cures based upon plants are still remembered and in
some cases still used. A cure for chilblains is to anoint them with an
ointment made from deadly-nightshade juice mixed with lard. The
juice squeezed from houseleek cures ear-ache. Houseleek growing on
the roof of a house is said to protect it from fire. Along the Gloucestershire border a fomentation of marshmallow leaves, soaked in
boiling water, is used for mumps or swollen glands.

There are several cures for rheumatism, one of the great scourges of the countryman. It can be cured or prevented by chewing parsley or celery, thrashing the affected part with stinging-nettles, eating young dandelion leaves mixed with vinegar or by carrying a dried potato, a nutmeg or a chestnut conker in the pocket.

A common remedy for gatherings and boils is to soak madonna-lily leaves in brandy and lay them on, first the rough side to draw out the poison and then the smooth side to heal.

There were many cures for warts of which one of the simplest is to bind sliced potatoes on them but the most popular of all is to find a wart-charmer. The people round Charlbury have resort to a successful wart-charmer in Mrs Eileen Claridge, whose evidence on ghost traditions I quoted in Chapter 6. Mrs Claridge's method is very simple but she does not profess to cure unless the patient had faith in her. She counts the number of warts, takes a stick – either ash or elder – and cuts a notch on it for each wart. Then she tells the patient to forget about the warts and expect that they will go. When she goes out to work she throws the stick with her right hand over her left shoulder without looking where it falls. She then puts it out of her mind. The district nurse and the doctor send patients to her and as a rule they are cured.

The Cotswold area awaits a Ewart Evans to do research on the horse-lore. The horse has left the farms, but the memory of it remains and there is much hunting and some local race meetings to keep the traditions of horsemanship alive. A Burford octogenarian told me in August of 1973 that her father, who was the local grazier, had a thousand acres of farmland and that her brothers rode to school every day, stabled their ponies at the White Horse and rode back at night. At that time there were three smiths in Burford; now they are hard to find and much in demand.

The few recorded pieces of horse-lore are very meagre. Here are a few recent ones: 'If mares slipped their foals, a black donkey would be run with them to cure the evil. If a donkey was unavailable then a goat could be used in the same way. Both these remedies have been used with success within living memory.' This was noted in Freeland. They say in Hook Norton, ' A good horse is never a bad colour', but this is a somewhat ambiguous saying. It may mean that if a horse is good the colour is immaterial, or it may mean that one can tell from its colour whether a horse is good or not. It is generally said that a white flash on the forehead is lucky and so is one white foot but a horse with four white feet should be avoided: it will be unlucky and will have a vicious temper.

Some horses are not necessarily unlucky to the rider but are ominous to meet. A white horse is the chief of these. On meeting a white horse it is thought wise to cross one's fingers and keep them crossed until one sees a dog. A dapple-grey horse is also rather unlucky but a piebald is lucky and anyone who sees a piebald horse without seeing its tail can obtain a wish. It is however said that he must not so much as think of its tail, which of course makes the success of the wish impossible.

The frequent presence of the hobby horse with the Morris dancers shows that there was an important horse tradition once. Spectral horses are usually drawing coaches in this part of the world. They sometimes breathe fire and have flaming eyes, like those drawing the Tanfield coach at Wilcote.

It is not long since the land in the Cotswolds was ploughed by oxen. The shoes worn by the plough oxen are to be seen in Filkins Folk Museum but only the very oldest people can remember seeing this method of ploughing and it is to be feared that the lore and traditions surrounding the custom have vanished out of living memory.

Sheep played an important part in Cotswold life and there are many stories of sheep-stealers, some of them banded into desperate gangs. Most of the beliefs about horses and sheep are widespread and not peculiar to the Cotswolds. Many of them relate to lambs and the lambing season but a few are about sheep and various folk remedies make use of sheep's dung or sheep's wool. Weather prognostications are drawn from their behaviour. It is said to be lucky to meet a flock on a journey. On the Welsh border the blade-bone of a sheep is used for divination and it is more widely used as a love spell to summon a lover, however unwilling, to his mistress. The rhyme that accompanies the action of pricking the blade-bone with a pin or a sharp knife is:

> It is not this bone I mean to stick
> But my love's heart I mean to prick
> Wishing him neither rest nor sleep
> Until he comes with me to speak.

This is supposed to cause great anguish to the lover, and is only used in desperation.

An even more widely used spell is that to break evil enchantments. All doors and windows are closed and a sheep's heart is stuck full of pins and set to roast and dry in the smoke of the fire. The witch will come in great agony to the door, must not be let in but must promise to take off the enchantment. This magic was occasionally used for revenge instead of for spell-breaking. Dried hearts stuck full of pins are sometimes found in old chimneys.

In Oxfordshire sheep's dung rolled into pills and swallowed was said to be healthful. As late as 1904 a cure for ague was to swallow a live sheep-tick for nine successive mornings.

In Christian times the lamb has been the symbol of Christ and many beliefs have been attached to it. It is a lucky omen for the flock if the first birth is of white twins and it is lucky if the first lamb seen in the year is looking towards one. Lamb pancakes, as they were called, used always to be given to the shepherd when the first lamb was dropped. This is still remembered by old people. In Chilson when the lambs' tails are docked they are given to the shepherd to make lambs'-tail pie. This is still done (1959). In Shipton-under-Wychwood they say that old-fashioned shepherds never dock lambs' tails when the moon is southing, that is on the wane. If they do the lambs will die.

Kirtlington in Oxfordshire is just on the verge of the Cotswolds and here, until 1858, a significant and ancient festival Kirtlington Lamb Ale, was held on Trinity Monday. The best lamb in the parish was chosen and carried about in procession decked with ribbons and treated with all honour, on the Monday and Tuesday. On Wednesday it was killed and its flesh cooked in luck-bringing pies which were distributed among the people free, except for the pie containing the head which was the luckiest of all. This had to be paid for. The ceremony may well have dated from pre-Christian times.

The number of black dogs and spectral dogs to be found in the Cotswolds is such as to deserve separate treatment in Chapter 11. Other dog beliefs, such as that dogs can see ghosts and spirits, that their howling portends death, that they can detect evil intentions against their masters and do their best to protect them, are to be found in the Cotswolds as elsewhere. A less common belief is that given by Aubrey: that a spayed bitch would protect a place against ghosts and spirits. Plot refers to this belief in his *History of Oxfordshire* when he is giving an account of the Haunting at Woodstock:

October 21. The Keeper of their *Ordnary* and his *Bitch*, lay in one of the *Rooms* with them, which Night they were not dis-

turbed at all. But *October* 22, though the *Bitch* kennel'd there
again (to whom they ascribed their former Nighte rest) both
They and the *Bitch* were in a pitiful taking; the *Bitch* opening
but once, and that with a *whining fearful* yelp.

Cats have been at the receiving end of a good deal of cruelty
because of their association with witches in popular belief but in the
Cotswolds we hear more of hares than of cats in the witch stories. A
black cat is generally thought lucky in this part of the world and a
white cat, like other white animals, is unlucky. People who have a
white cat sometimes counteract it with a black one. It is a good
omen if a strange black cat comes into the house and it should not
be driven away. It is of course lucky if a black cat crosses one's path
and particularly the path of a bridal party. Kittens born in May
are thought to be uncanny and to have a habit of carrying snakes
into the house. If the cat deserts the house at a time of illness, it is
thought that the patient will die.

Hares are the subject of a great many superstitions. It was one of
the chief forms that witches were supposed to assume, partly because
of the strange frolics of hares at the courting season and the 'hares'
parliament' which appears to be a matter of actual observation, and
partly perhaps because their scuts are so short. It used to be thought
that a witch could transform herself member for member but could
not take the form of a tailed animal. This belief is referred to in
Macbeth but is not universal; it was more generally believed that
a witch could take any form but that of a lamb or a dove.

The fox also has a popular association with witches, who are
supposed occasionally to turn themselves into foxes. David Garnett's
Lady into Fox has therefore some folk foundation – at Kirtlington
at the end of the nineteenth century one old woman was supposed
to have this power. A fine vixen was often hunted near her house
but was never caught. Once the hounds got so close that it seemed
impossible that the fox could get away but it made a sudden turn
and escaped into the old woman's house. A few seconds later the
huntsmen followed it. They saw nothing but the old woman sitting
quietly beside her fire.

Rats and mice have strong magical associations and many legends
are told about them. If rats suddenly leave a house without any
measures having been taken against them it is said to portend a
death in the family and the same is true of mice, though a sudden
infestation of mice is also ominous. Mice are also used in cures. In

1936 an Oxfordshire woman said that whooping-cough could be cured by frying the flesh of a mouse, skinned and boned, and giving it to the patient. She said that it was quite appetising and that the patient need not know what it was.

Bees used to play a great part in rural economy and were much respected. The necessity of keeping them abreast with family news and especially with the news of a death has been already mentioned. Bee stings were said to be a cure for rheumatism. Butterflies had from early times a strong connection with the soul and they were also omens of good and ill. In Gloucestershire it used to be said that if the first butterfly seen was a white one it meant that white bread would be eaten all the year; if it was a brown one nothing but brown bread could be expected. This was supposed to mark the difference between prosperity and poverty.

Of all birds robins seem from the sixteenth century onwards to be the most beloved. To kill a robin or even to rob a robin's nest is thought wicked and dangerous by even the wildest schoolboys. Everyone likes to have a robin in the garden but its very sacredness makes it ominous. A robin tapping on a window pane is thought to be a death token. In Gloucestershire and Oxfordshire a robin entering the house is equally ominous, except, for some reason, in the month of November, when it is lucky. In Oxfordshire a robin singing near the house foretells bad news and one perching on the chair where someone is sitting foretells that person's death. In Lechlade in 1950 a Christmas card with a robin on it was thought to be unlucky. This cannot be a widespread belief, or Christmas cards with robins on them would not be so frequently sent.

Although ravens are unlucky, people generally welcome rooks near their house and the sudden desertion of a rookery is thought to be ominous. They are supposed to be knowing and the desertion of an elm tree by the nesting birds is taken to mean that the tree will soon fall. There may be some observation behind this belief, for one of the sisters in the priory at Burford was walking in the wood there when the rooks were building and suddenly all the rooks fell upon one half-built nest and tore it to pieces. A few minutes later there was a great crash and the limb on which the nest had been built fell to the ground.

Many other creatures as well as rooks were supposed to be weather-wise. A pleasant collection of weather signs was given in the annual record of the Oxford Folklore Society in 1953:

When thrushes keep near the hedges, and wagtails keep near farm-buildings, when the green woodpecker whistles and peacocks screech, when cattle face all one way and lie down on low pastures, when rabbits come out by day and feed in large numbers, and donkeys bray loudly, rain is coming.

When a summer morning is misty and cows climb to high ground, when sheep lie down all together and rest peacefully, and frogs' skins are bright and yellow, it will be fine.

I

10 Witches in the Cotswolds

THERE SEEM TO HAVE BEEN no formal prosecutions for witchcraft through the whole Cotswold area, none even in the time when the witchcraft hysteria was at its height. In Oxfordshire no records of witch trials are to be found and those few in Gloucestershire were in Gloucester and Bristol, outside the Cotswold area. It is true that there was no main country town in the Cotswolds at which assizes were held but we do not hear of witch prosecutions set on foot, or of lynch law. And this was at a time, as we have seen, when many brutalities were committed and when rough music was a common outlet for popular disapproval. The most notorious act of violence committed against a witch was that of a single crazed man, James of Long Compton, a labourer, who in 1875 assaulted a neighbour, an old woman of 80, believing her to be a witch. It was a September evening and he was going home from a day of reaping in the fields, his weak head much affected by the gallon of beer he had drunk, mixed with a quantity of raw, heady cider. He had lately suffered from pains, cramps and swollen legs and was convinced that they had been brought on by the witches who were supposed to swarm in Long Compton. Some altercation seems to have arisen between him and his old neighbour and he suddenly slashed her over the head with his sickle. This was probably an attempt to 'draw her blood above the breath' which was the standard method of destroying a witch's power but the poor old woman was knocked down by the blow and the pain, shock and loss of blood killed her. Even then the shock of her death did not rouse the poor man from his delusion. James declared that he had been bewitched by her and prevented from doing his work properly. There were 16 more witches like her in the village, he said, and they should all have been treated in the same way. Through the trial he stood, silent and dazed, a little, dull man, five foot four inches in height. The barrister defending him did so on the grounds that he believed himself to be in danger from witchcraft and acted, as he thought, in self-defence. It is probably the last time that such a defence was brought before a jury.

But though he was silent and dazed at his trial James was ready to talk to the superintendent of the police and told him that the water given him to drink was full of witches and would get inside him. He talked of how horses and cattle had sickened and died under the Evil Eye and ascribed all the local misfortunes to the ill-will of the witches. According to the remarks made at the inquest he was not solitary in his opinions – they were shared by many of his neighbours. Though he was pronounced guilty at his trial James was not condemned to death because he was believed to be insane but was detained at the Queen's pleasure. He was so much possessed by the fear of witches, however, that he would neither eat nor drink, and soon pined away and died.

Another witch belief that occurred in a legal context was the mysterious case of Mr Harrison, mentioned in Chapter 7. Joan Perry appears to have been considered a witch, even at the time of her trial, and may have been the more readily condemned for that reason by R. Hyde, an inexperienced and ill-qualified judge, hastily appointed in 1660 to fill the places of those commissioned in the Protectorate who had no legal standing. In the pamphlets and the ballad from Anthony Wood's collection it is said that Joan Perry was afterwards discovered to be a witch. In the preface to the ballad we find:

It now appears the Widow Perry was a witch, and after her Sons had robd him, and cast him into a Stone Pit, she by her witchcraft conveyed him upon a Rock in the Sea near Turky, where he remained four days and nights, till a Turkish Ship coming by took him and sold him into Turky, where he remained for a season, but is now through the good providence of God returned again safe to England, to the great wonder and admiration of all that know the same.

Or as the ballad itself puts it:

> But lest that any of this truth should doubt,
> Ile tell you how this business came about.
> This Widow *Pery* as tis plainly shown
> Was then a Witch although it was not known.
>
> So when these Villains by their mothers aid
> Had knockt him down (even as before was said)
> They took away his money every whit,
> And then his body cast into a pit.
>
> He scarce was come unto himself before
> Another wonder did amaze him more,
> That whilst he lookt about, he found that he
> Was suddenly conveyed unto the sea.
>
> First on the shore he stood a little space
> And thence unto a rock transported was,
> Where he four days and nights did then remain
> And little thought to see his friends again.

Wild and unconvincing as this story is, it seems almost rational in comparison with Mr Harrison's own account of being carried bound on horseback from Chipping Campden to Deal in Kent, after having been twice wounded, robbed of his money and a fresh supply of money crammed into his pockets. The ballad ends:

> Let not this seem incredible to any,
> Because it is an end apprised by many,
> This is no feigned story, though tis new,
> But as tis very strange tis very true.

You see how far a Witches power extends,
When as to wickedness her mind she bends;
Great is her Malice, yet can God restrain her,
And at his pleasure let her loose or chain her.

If God had let her work her utmost spight,
No doubt she would have kild the man outright,
But he is saved and she for all her malice,
Was very justly hang'd upon the Gallows.

Then let all praise to God alone be given,
By men on earth as by the saints in heaven,
He by his mercy dayly doth befriend us,
And by his power he will still defend us.

The pamphlet, printed in 1662, followed the same story. Anthony Wood had a copy of Overbury's account of the mystery and also of the ballad, though not of the pamphlet. On the tail-page of the Overbury quarto he made some notes:

John Perry hung in chains on the same gallows. Richard and Joan Perry were after execution taken down and buried under the gallows. Three days after a gentle-woman pretending to understand witches hired a man to dig up the grave that she might search Joan's body – she being on horseback drew up to the grave which was opened but the horse, starting at the sight of the body in the grave, ran away under the gallows and her head hitting against John's feet struck her off from the horse into the grave.

A later note to the pamphlet written by John Gough in 1780 was supposed to depend on the information of a Mr Barnsley of Charringworth, which gives a possibly later development of the witch legend:

Mr Harrison's wife fell into a deep melancholy and at last hanged herself after the return of her husband; after her death there was found a letter in her scrutore which she had received from her husband, dated before the execution of Joan and her two sons. There was a report that Joan had bewitched a woman that lay bedridden several years, who upon her execution got up and recovered her former state of health.

Anthony Wood also mentions Mrs Harrison's suicide, describing her with his usual unkindness as a 'snotty covetous presbyterian'.

These are two examples of the law in some relation to witches and it is possible that the legend of Nan's Tump, mentioned in Chapter 1, of a witch buried standing upright may be a trace of a mob demonstration against a witch but it is too vague to be informative. Most of the stories of witches, though they illustrate various aspects of witch belief, are not vindictive.

The legend of the Rollright Stones gives us an early example of the elder as a witch tree as well as the witch's power, usually belonging either to saints or to the Devil, of turning people into stone. The almost contemporary tale told by Mrs Falconer and given in Chapter 6 is remarkable for its tolerance. Although the old woman would be considered responsible for the death of her baby, Rhoda went to nurse her in her last illness. In this tale there is evidence of the belief in the diabolic compact. There was a tale of shape-shifting told about another reputed witch among Mrs Falconer's acquaintance but Mrs Falconer was sceptical about this and said that the woman was always a good neighbour. A fuller story of shape-shifting is told by Edward Rainsberry in *Through the Lych Gate*:

There is a story told that many years ago three young lads from Long Compton named Will, Jack and Lewis were out netting rabbits down by Barton's Grove. They saw a white hare run behind a hedge, then a little later running in circles across a gateway. The lads carried on with their trapping, but every time they looked up the hare seemed to be drawing nearer to them in decreasing circles. Despite the moon it was now getting dark, so they decided to finish for the night and get along home. Following the footpath back through the fields, they looked round – the hare was following them. When they stopped, it stopped; when they ran, it ran also. Eventually they were running as fast as they could and got back to the village across Duffus Close. One of the lads lived in a cottage on the main road, so the three jumped across the stone wall into his back garden. He tried to open the back door but the key would not fit; glancing round before he forced the door open, he saw the white hare sitting on the garden wall.

A hare was one of the forms most commonly supposed to be taken by a witch; all white animals were thought to be uncanny and a white hare would almost certainly be a witch. The courting dances of the hares, like the courting dances of the blackcock, brought down on them a suspicion of magical practices.

They used to say, ' There are enough witches in Long Compton to draw a load of hay up Long Compton Hill ' and this was said until well into the twentieth century. One Long Compton witch was supposed to ride up the old road in a cheese kibber. The neighbouring villages of Brailes, Tysoe and Ilmington were also supposed to be the haunts of witches.

I was once told a witch story about Poulton crossroads at the Cirencester end of the Cotswolds. One arm of the sign-post directs one to ' Betty's Grave ' and there close at hand is a well-marked grave-mound. There are two stories about Betty. One is that she wagered that she would reap an acre of corn with her own sickle within a certain time. She won her wager but fell down dead at the end of it and was buried where she fell; the other, that she was a Poulton woman who poisoned herself and was buried at the nearest cross-roads. Whichever tale was true – and the second seems the more likely – a cross-roads grave is an irresistible invitation to witches. My informant, a member of the Burford old people's club, who had lived near Poulton, told me that the local witches used to amuse themselves by holding up the pedlars on their way to Fairford market. They would keep them there all day, unable to move, and would release them in the evening when it was too late to sell their goods. The usual means of halting a horse was to stick crossed pins into a gateway or post. My informant said that the witches were all dead now but she seemed to believe that their ghosts still haunt the cross-roads.

A childhood acquaintance with a village witch came up into the memory of Mrs Haynes, one of the Wallers of Burford to whom I have been indebted for a good many local legends and traditions. In her old age she had to be taken to a nursing home in Cheltenham and her daughter, Renée Haynes, was good enough to send me this note:

When she was a child of 6 or 7, staying near Dowdeswell (close to Whittington Court, I gathered) she used to go down the village, and sometimes met an old woman, who was quite clean and tidy, and very nice to her (' Come out of the sun, missy, you'll get sunstroke', that sort of remark) but could be extremely unpleasant if crossed. My mother's nurse said the old woman was a witch and should be avoided; when my mother started singing a little tune that she had overheard the witch singing, the nurse was shocked and alarmed, and said she must never do so again, as that was the tune the witch used to summon her demon. I asked how it went, and she said TING, TING, TING, TING-TANG TING, and that someone else's television, which she could hear through the wall playing pop music had brought the whole thing back to her memory (rather unpleasantly, I gathered).

One can see that the old woman's politeness and solicitude would be suspect as a means of laying the evil eye on the child. The danger positively mentioned might well be invoked by the threat. One can see well the loneliness that these suspect witches had to suffer, however immune they might be from attacks by legal processes.

A parallel to this fear of a witch song is given by Ruth Tongue in *Somerset Folklore*. Ruth Tongue and her play-fellows were always stopped by the old women of the village from playing ' Sally Go Round the Moon' which was supposed to be a witch game.

Angelina Parker recalls an experience rather like Mrs Haynes' in a paper in *Folklore*:

I remember an old woman called ' Shaking Charlotte', who was afflicted with palsy, and we were always told she was a witch, and the children used to run away when they saw her coming, but I never heard that she did any harm. If you could scratch the supposed witch with a pin and fetch blood, she was unable to harm you. An old lady once told me that, many years before, she was in a low, depressed state of mind, and her brother came to see her. He said solemnly – ' Jane, you're bewitched. I'll tell you what I will do. I will pin a cross over your door, and then no unholy thing can enter in.' He then placed two straws in the shape of a cross over the doorway. She did recover, but whether in consequence of the cross or not she could not say.

My mother used to speak of a boy who was supposed to be bewitched. She told me his name, but I have forgotten it. It was said that he would run straight up the walls of houses, and over the roof like a cat.

In all these anecdotes of witchcraft there is no real narrative, unless we make an exception for the elder-tree witch of the Rollright Stones. There is no story like those of the Lancashire Witches, nor of Blind Byard and the Witch; nothing too of the dramatic witch stories of Scotland, the Witches of Delnado nor Isobel Gowdie's and Major Weir's confessions, nor chapbook tales like the Witch of the Woodlands, nor grim medieval tales like the Witch of Berkeley or the Witch of Fordham. East and west and north and south there are fiercer, grimmer tales and yet most of the qualities and activities of the witches are hinted at in these brief legends. There is a hint of witches' meetings above Long Compton, of the witch's power to injure men and beasts in the crazy attack of James the labourer. In Long Compton too, as well as in Wychwood, we have the shape-shifting stories. We have the raising of a familiar spirit in the Dowdeswell witch and the witch marks made by the familiars looked for by the officious woman in the Chipping Campden case. There is the compact with the Devil and his gift of money in the tale of the Witch's Purse, besides the power over a child's life. In the Chipping Campden story the witch's power of transporting other people as well as herself is taken for granted. The boy who ran up walls was probably supposed to be possessed by a devil. There happens to be no mention of a witch travelling by broomstick, though there is one who prefers to travel in a cheese-kibble. One interesting example of a witch-sending, in which a demon or poltergeist is wished on someone who had insulted a witch, is given by R. R. Marett in an article in Volume 44 of *Folklore* called 'the Little Tew Ghost'. It is reminiscent of the famous seventeenth-century case of the Demon Drummer of Tedworth.

There has come into my hands a small pamphlet, published in 1854, referring to events that happened during the years 1838–39, entitled *Personal Recollections of Little Tew Ghost*, by Edgar Hewlett, described as 'Minister of the Gospel' and presumably not belonging to the Church of England. It concerns a young person called Hannah. One day an old woman called at the door and offered to tell Hannah's fortune. The latter reproved the unwelcome visitor, saying that she was an imposter; but thereat the old woman, greatly enraged, said that she *would* tell her fortune, which was that she should be married within the next three months to a young man, of whose person she gave some description. As soon as she was gone, Hannah discovered 'something very ugly resembling an eft or asker' hanging upon her gown, which caused her so violent a fit that she had to leave her situation and reside with her relatives. Thereupon, sure enough, she met a respectable young man and was duly married within the time prophesied. Later on, after she had had a baby, it became apparent that she was 'suffering both in mind and body from some invisible agency.' For instance, 'unearthly sounds were heard to proceed from various parts of the house.' Sometimes it was as a scratching noise, at other times as a moaning sound, and frequently as a shrill whistle.

At length this evil one appeared to grow more bold, and played all the tricks of the poltergeist. Hannah's medicine bottle, for instance, was dashed out of her hand, or her apron was twitched off, or something thumped the bedroom floor. Worst of all, the thing had the habit of taking off her wedding-ring and hiding it. In fact 'it had become quite a familiar spirit in the house,' and could constantly be heard 'using very vulgar language and sometimes swearing dreadfully.' Letters on the subject filled the Oxford newspapers, one of them stating 'that the Rector and Fellows of Exeter College, Oxford (to whom Little Tew belongs) were about to use means for the speedy removal of the troublesome one.' I am not able, however, in my official capacity to state that anything was done, and, to be frank, I am not sure, if such a case were to present itself to-day, how the College would proceed. Indeed, those who attempted to interfere were usually worsted. 'A strong, hearty widow woman who kept a public house in the village said she was determined to be satisfied about the matter . . . How great was her surprise when she was lifted from the floor towards the ceiling and again replaced upon her feet without sustaining any injury to her person.' Again 'a respectable man, a draper by trade, visited the cottage' and asked innocently 'Is this the stool it has thrown at persons?' Instantly the stool in question 'was thrown against his leg by an invisible hand with much violence; and he observed, "I shall never forget it."' Persons of scientific leanings even hired a ventriloquist, at the price of £10, to see if he could reproduce the unearthly sounds, but, although 'eminent in his profession', he failed to do so.

To cut a long story short, the Rev. Mr Hewlett has to intervene. Facing ' the indescribable sound ', he was shocked to hear something exclaim in a ' loud sepulchral voice, " You're a fool." ' Nevertheless, he exorcised it in due form and Hannah cried, ' I do think he is driven away.' And indeed he was.

Perhaps the very wildness and remoteness of the Cotswolds prevented accusations of witchcraft from being made. It was believed in the sixteenth and seventeenth centuries that witches lost their power when they fell into the hands of the law. In many places in the Cotswolds the law was not immediately available; perhaps it was felt to be safer to keep on good terms with the local witches. In spite of the scattered and scanty evidence there is little doubt that there was a widespread and genuine belief in witchcraft.

11 Supernatural Beliefs

THE OLD SAYING ' as sure as God's in Gloucestershire' may be said
to have come into operation in banishing traditions of the Devil
from the Cotswolds, for they are rare. In the Severn and Thames
valleys and the plain of Gloucester they are commoner. We have
the horrific devil who carried off the Witch of Berkeley, the Devil's
Chapel in the Forest of Dean, the Devil's Quoits near Stanton Har-
court, a good though undocumented version of the Devil as a hunter
of souls told by Kenneth Hare in *Gloucestershire*, one of the
'County Books' series. This is a version of Mrs Bray's Devonshire
story in which a hare who is the ghost of a witch takes refuge in a
market woman's basket and is saved forever from the Devil and his
hounds because they pass by and she sees their tails. In Mrs Bray's
story, and in Ruth Tongue's variant from Somerset, she is an old
woman; in Kenneth Hare's she is a young and pretty girl on her
way to Gloucester market. Where she started from is not told –

it may have been from Stroud. It is hardly fair to cite it as a Cotswold tale. It is told as an example of Gloucestershire dialect and it is possible that Kenneth Hare translated a tale already familiar to him from his native West Country.

The Cotswolds are sprinkled with standing stones but none of them are directly named from the Devil. Witches have acted as his deputy, as in the legend of the Rollright Stones, or ghosts have taken over the function of the Devil's coach. As we shall see, there are plenty of carvings of devils in Cotswold churches and lively Hell scenes in the painted 'Dooms' but not many houses are directly haunted by the Devil. Angelina Parker in her *North Leigh Folklore* says that Hill Farm, which had a priest's hole in it, was haunted by the Devil as well as by ghosts. One man who lived there became suddenly rich and it was supposed that he had found the ghost's treasure. A man called Jack Adams claimed to have seen the Devil near Hill Farm and said he was 'all spotted and speckled'. So the saying arose in North Leigh, 'All spotted and speckled like Jack Adams' Devil'. The humorous tale of the Devil on Birdlip Hill comes just on the edge of the Cotswolds.

North Leigh, however, seems to have been his most popular haunt. An article on 'The Devil in Oxfordshire', signed 'E.C.' and published in the 1952 *Annual Report of the Oxfordshire and District Folklore Society*, gives several examples from North Leigh. He was likely to appear to North Leigh sabbath-breakers. If anyone goes nutting on a Sunday the Devil joins them and pulls down the branches within easy reach. Nutting is always a perilous pastime and girls indulge in it to the hazard of their maidenhood. Once some men caught a badger on a Sunday and put it in a bag but on the way home it disappeared, leaving a strong smell of brimstone. One day some boys were playing Sunday cricket on the common when they were joined by a stranger, an excellent player. At the end of the game he vanished in a cloud of smoke. There is a tomb with a hole in it on the north side – the Devil's side – of North Leigh church. Anyone who runs round it 12 times and looks through the hole will see the Devil. The village children used to begin running round but their courage usually failed before the 12th time. One girl of 18, however said in 1934 that she had run the full 12 times round and looked in and seen nothing. Perhaps she had gone sunwise instead of widershins.

Angelina Parker had a few things to say about the Devil in her contribution to *Folklore* on 'Oxfordshire Village Folklore':

There were many stories of the Devil (familiarly spoken of as 'Old Nick' or 'Old Scrat') appearing to people. A man was going from Northleigh to Barnard Gate, and the Devil came to him in the shape of a fiery serpent, and surrounded him so that he could not pass for some hours. When at length he was able to make his escape, he went back to Northleigh and brought several friends to the place where the serpent had been, but it had disappeared.

If for some reason you should wish to call up the Devil you should say the Lord's Prayer backwards. If a girl looks a long time in the looking-glass admiring herself, the Devil will come behind her and look over her shoulder. Any particularly profane or wicked person was said to have sold his soul to the Devil.

The three beautiful churches of Adderbury, Bloxham and King's Sutton are said to have been built with the Devil's help. Three brothers were the builders and they were joined by an unknown workman of uncanny skill. He was finally recognised as the Devil because one day he stumbled with his huge load. A pile of mortar shot out of his hod and became Crouch Hill.

Fairies and domestic spirits, which must have been pretty active in that region, have almost completely disappeared, although they are supposed to be responsible for the transport of Tackley church from its intended site. The last recorded sight of them, as I have said earlier, was around the King-Stone of the Rollright Stones – appropriately near to Warwickshire. Two more recent tales of fairies are included in Chapter 5 but they may well date from the same period. Ghosts and black dogs have taken over all the functions of supernatural beings, even sometimes of ancient gods. The Tanfields, who managed to spread their unpopularity over an extraordinarily wide area, are an example of this.

Laurence Tanfield had been born in Burford in relatively poor circumstances but his mother managed to have him educated for the Law and his own industry, drive and covetousness advanced him in wealth and dignity. He became sergeant at law, a judge and finally Lord Chief Baron. He purchased and rebuilt Burford Priory and in 1617 he bought the lordship of the manor and became the first resident lord of the manor since the Norman Conquest. During those 550 years the citizens of Burford had come to regard it as a royal borough but they were soon to learn their mistake. In 1620 a *quo warranto* was brought against the burgesses of Burford by the

Attorney-General and tried in a court presided over by Sir Laurence Tanfield. By its ruling the burgesses were stripped of the rights which they had assumed and a few to which they were entitled. It is not hard to imagine that the new lord of the manor became exceedingly unpopular in Burford and his wife, who was harsher and more grinding than he was, became more unpopular still. She was alleged to have said that she would have liked to grind the Burford people to powder beneath her chariot wheels and it was in a chariot that she subsequently haunted the place. In Great Tew, where the exactions were made without so much legal justification, she was equally hated. In Whittington, where he possessed another manor, Sir Laurence was hated and for some reason their reputation was equally bad at Wilcote near North Leigh. Lady Tanfield, who survived her husband by a few years, seems to have made the deepest impression on Burford. She was said to ride over the roofs of the town in a fiery chariot, sometimes with Sir Laurence, foretelling any misfortune likely to overtake the town. In the eighteenth century she became so troublesome that a band of clergymen, sometimes said to be 4, sometimes 7 and sometimes 12, came together to lay her. They succeeded in calling her into the church and conjuring her into a bottle which they corked securely before throwing her into the river under the first arch of the bridge. It was believed that in times of drought, if the Windrush under that arch ran dry, Lady Tanfield would rise again and once more ride over the roofs of Burford. Mrs Groves, recording some of her father's reminiscences at the end of *The History of Shipton-under-Wychwood* gives some details of the Tanfield haunting and Sir Laurence has his part in it, though Lady Tanfield is usually the sole agent in the tale. She says:

Old Dame Taylor, my grandmother's nurse, told father that Lord and Lady Tanfield used to drive over the roofs of the Burford houses – up one side of the street and down the other. This became such a nuisance that the townspeople got seven clergymen to come and 'lay' them under Burford Bridge – *the first arch* – seven priests with bell, book and candle. If ever the arch gets dry they will come again. One dry season it began to 'hiss and bubble', so the people watered it till the river rose.

The story of the laying of the ghost was known beyond Burford, for old Mrs Falconer of Leafield told me in the 1960s of the conjuring into a bottle – a detail forgotten in the Burford version. It was said also to be Lady Tanfield's ghost that haunted Great Tew, though that story may be now forgotten. Mrs Haynes' legend of the Wicked Lord's Lane has been given in Chapter 5. Here Sir Laurence may be said to have taken the place of the Devil in many of the West Country folk legends, just as some shadow of the tradition of Hecla's Hell Wain hangs over the Burford account of Lady Tanfield's activities. So far the couple have worked separately, though always in coaches, but Angelina Parker reports a joint operation. In her ' Folklore Notes ' of 1923 she says that the ghosts of Lord and Lady Tanfield were reported to drive from Wilcote to North Leigh, with flames and smoke coming from their horses' nostrils. An old North Leigh man said he had seen them and the horse he was driving, although blind, trembled and broke into a lather.

These spectral coaches are fairly common in the Cotswolds. It will be remembered that Mrs Falconer described seeing one as a girl when going with her mother through the forest, and Mr Bayliss's father was apparently quite accustomed to one passing him at midnight near the Sarsden Stones. Sir William and Lady Wilcote were also credited with coach riding. Apparently they were supposed to have taken to it – a distinct innovation for medieval people – in annoyance because Sir Laurence Tanfield had diverted a charity left by Sir William for the poor of Wilcote to his own uses. Sir George Cobb of Cobb Hall, Adderbury, who was drowned in 1672, occasionally appeared in a coach with fire-breathing horses. He once frightened some poachers so much that they never poached again.

The method of laying a ghost by conjuration is also fairly common, as we can see in Mrs Groves' account of the laying of Sir John Reade. The Wilcote ghost was also laid by conjuration but the bell and clapper is an original feature. There are several versions of this ghost and its laying. We have already had Mrs Claridge's in Chapter 6. According to her the ghost was a black dog. Two bird-scaring clappers were used and one was thrown into each pond. There was a single priest and also a mother with a new-born child – presumably just christened, for a christened child is potent against the Devil. In Angelina Parker's account the laying was by several clergymen. A bell and clapper were separated, the bell put in one pool and the clapper in another. There was no mention of the presence of a child. Mrs Pratley of Wilcote, interviewed in May 1973, had heard of the Wilcote ghost from her grandmother. She said that the ghost was laid by 7 or 12 clergymen. One stood in the middle and the rest formed a ring round him. They said to the ghost, 'Wherefore troublest thou us?' To which the ghost replied, 'I shall haunt as long as the clapper and bell hang together.' They melted down the bell and put the clapper into the pond. In these various accounts there is no indication of the origin of the ghost. Though called a ghost it may possibly have been a devil since there was said to be a devil at Hill Farm and, according to Mrs Claridge, the haunting was in the form of a black dog and a new-born child was used to lay it.

Mr George Pratley, also of Wilcote, had not heard of this ghost but remembered another, that which haunted one room in Wilcote Manor. He had known a man who was courting the squire's daughter and who was given the haunted room to sleep in. It seems that he suspected practical jokes, for he moved the chest of drawers across the bedroom door before he got into bed. He spent an undisturbed night but in the morning the chest of drawers had been moved back to its former place. The furniture-moving ghosts are generally poltergeist manifestations, which would account for the comparatively short duration of this haunting. Mr Pratley said that the squire had offered money to anyone who would sleep in the room but he did not think that the offer had been accepted.

Almost every village or small town in the Cotswolds seems to have several ghosts attached to it, though they are often unidentified hauntings. Mrs Claridge's account of the ghost who haunted one of the Wychwood ponds has been given in Chapter 6, and so has Mrs Falconer's experience with the Fairspeare ghost and Mr Andrews' description of the ghosts of Swinbrook.

One ghostly appearance which has a well-documented historical foundation is that on a piece of land called Stonefield on the small road between Asthall and Brize Norton. In the 1930s a deserted farmhouse, in a very pleasant seventeenth-century style like a miniature manor house, stood there. A most unpleasant story was attached to it. In the seventeenth century a woman lived there who practised the trade of baby-farming. Merchants' daughters and superior servant maids who had got into trouble went there to have their babies and provided sums of money for their maintenance and subsequent apprenticeship. In Thomas Heywood's play *The Wise Woman of Hogsden* the usual routine is described but the Wise Woman was more conscientious than the mistress of Stonefield – she provided godparents for the children and arranged for their apprenticeship. This baby-farmer, however, accepted the money but murdered the

K

babies and buried their little bodies in her garden. At length her crimes caught up with her and she was hanged. No one cared to inhabit the house and it was used as a pest-house in the eighteenth-century smallpox epidemic. In the 1940s it was pulled down and now only the barn remains to mark the place. But even after the house was gone, people going along that road at midnight were supposed to see a lantern moving about where the garden had been, as the ghost of the murderess buried her victims. Curiously enough, this story seems to have moved to Burford and to have been told about the wife of one of the vicars, the Rev. John Thorpe, who was said to have taken in children, disposed of them and buried them in the vicarage garden. It even moved one step farther and was attached without any plausibility at all to the children carved on the Harmon tomb.

Here is a shifting ghost story but there is also a story in Burford of a shifting ghost. In the nineteenth century there were a number of small cottages standing at the back of High Street and of Sheep Street, which have since fallen into disrepair and been pulled down. Three of these stood in what was afterwards Wiggins Yard to the west of High Street. The cottage furthest to the west was very badly haunted, so badly that nobody would occupy it and it fell into ruins. Apparently the ghost found it untenable too, for it moved into the next cottage and then into the next and, when all three houses had been abandoned, into the house in the High Street on which the row of cottages abutted. Here it was encountered by my informant, a member of the Women's Institute whose family had moved into Burford from the country and who was very proud, as a girl in her early teens, to have a room all to herself. She soon found the noises and other sensations around her unbearable and got her young brother to sleep with her. He was equally terrified. It seems to have been a kind of poltergeist haunting, with pushing and pulling and flinging of objects as well as noises. The mother was at first unsympathetic but soon also witnessed the haunting. The father was always sceptical and experienced nothing. That room was abandoned and was only once used when an uncle and aunt, who also complained of the noises, came to stay. The hauntings went on as long as the family stayed there. Another member of the Institute had lived in it later but said the noises were only those of rats.

This is a specimen of the ghost stories told in Burford. Ten more have been narrated to me at various times and are of varying degrees of authenticity. All these tales are from one small town and it is likely that anyone residing for 40 years or so anywhere in the Cotswolds would be able to rival them.

Many of the hauntings that I have described are those of wicked souls that could not rest; others are of those who have suffered a violent death, such as the headless sixteenth-century gentleman who joined Mr Bayliss senior on his midnight walks. An equally common cause of haunting is said to be that of treasure or metal hidden undisclosed before death.

An example of this is given by William Monk in his *Walks and Drives Round Burford* (1896). The farm described is near Filkins. Near this house is Peacock Farm, so named because there are two yew trees in the garden which are trained in the shape of a peacock. The villagers tell a curious story in connection with the house. Years ago this farm was hired by a Mr Jonas Bassett. His housekeeper was named Betty Hill and she used to declare that a lady, in the garb of other days, frequently passed through the house. For years the apparition came, till one day some children, by playing rather boisterously in the old house, caused an old stocking to fall down from a place where it had been hidden away. In this old stocking, the story continues, there was a knob of gold, which is said to be of considerable value. It is satisfactory to be able to record that after this incident nothing was ever afterwards seen of the unhappy lady who had haunted Peacock Farm so long.

The usual result of finding hidden treasure is to lay the unquiet ghost but a tradition of North Leigh church to be found in the next chapter is of treasure that must not be disturbed.

Black dog hauntings, particularly those of demonic dogs, are not as common in the Cotswolds as in Suffolk, Yorkshire or the West Country but a few have already been mentioned: the haunting in Black Dog Lane near Fairspeare, the black dog of Birdlip Hill and the Wilcote black dog. The black dog that is said to haunt a ditch near Westwell is supposed to be the ghost of a real dog, a keeper's black retriever who was killed by poachers.

Black-Stockings is sometimes regarded as a goblin figure. According to Angelina Parker he was a headless ghost who carried his head and was in the habit of swarming up on to the coach and sitting beside the coachman. The passengers, she said, were at first terrified but became accustomed to the invasion.

The wife of a late vicar of Adderbury told me that the vicarage there was haunted by a ghost so sinister that their dog died of fright. Before the vicar left Adderbury he asked the churchwardens to have the house exorcised if the new vicar had children. The present vicar, however, denies that there is any haunting. The near-by vicarage of Deddington was said, according to Peter Underwood's *Gazetteer of British Ghosts*, to have been haunted for some time by the spirit of the vicar who died in 1962.

After citing these traditional pieces of rumour it is perhaps of interest to mention three experiences which might have sprouted into ghost stories but for immediate investigation. The late Mr Frank Pearman of Fulbrook told me that as a young man, at the beginning of this century, he had been walking across to Swinbrook by the field path passing Widford church, at that time derelict and not yet restored. It was dark and he saw something white moving in the overgrown churchyard. He went up to it at once and found that it was a red and white cow, grazing round the grave stones. Many a man would have hurried by, convinced that the uncanny spot was haunted.

A more amusing experience befell Mr Hill of Charlbury. He was bicycling home one night past the old Gospel Oak on the outskirts of Wychwood Forest when a woman cycling in front of him swerved wildly, screamed, dropped her bicycle and went into hysterics. He rode up quickly and dismounted. 'The ghost! The ghost!' she said, and he saw something white and wavy coming from behind the oak and heard deep pantings. He did his best to revive and comfort the poor woman and finally left both their bicycles and supported her down the road to the nearest house. Then he went back for the bicycles. The white wavy movement was still going on and the thing was still panting behind the oak, so Mr Hill went up to investigate it. Behind the oak stood a steam-roller. The roadmen had banked down the fires in the evening but a breeze had got up, the fires had burned through the slack and the roller was panting and smoking. A very pretty story of the Demon of the Oak was nipped in the bud by his courageous investigation.

A third rather eerie experience was told me by Mrs Falconer, to whom I am indebted for so many genuine pieces of folk tradition. At one time she used to go once a week to Chipping Norton to do some business there and one winter evening the shopman asked her how she was going to get home. She told him that she was walking. 'You shouldn't do that,' he said. 'You shouldn't go through the forest alone. Nothing would induce me to go through the forest again after dark.' And he told her the experience he had had some weeks ago.

He had been in the forest area collecting some debts and it had fallen dark, but he knew the track and had set out for home. As he walked he heard a rustling along the path and a figure came towards him that sighed and muttered. He was startled and stepped back out of the track and it passed quite close to him, sighing and muttering in an uncanny way. He let it pass and then ventured back on to the track but he had not gone very far before he heard the sighing and muttering again, this time behind him. He dashed off the track and looked for another way home but he lost both his way and one shoe in the mud and wandered round in circles, scratched and torn, until daybreak.

In spite of this daunting tale Mrs Falconer had no choice but to walk home and she reached the forest after sunset. When she was well into the forest she heard the muttering and sighing that the shopman had described. She prudently drew back from the path because she did not wish to be accosted by an unknown man and the figure passed her – but she recognised it as flesh and blood. It was an old labourer, known to her, who had been superannuated and moved into another cottage to make room for the new labourer and his family. The old man was homesick for the house he had lived in most of his life and would turn up in the evenings and spend the night sitting by what used to be his own fireside. He was senile and would talk and mutter to himself. The new tenants got tired of him and used to lock the door and pretend to be in bed and he would come back again and again to knock. It is as sad a tale as any ghost story and might have ended in one, but there was a healthy vein of scepticism in Mrs Falconer which made her a valuable witness.

The most compelling of all the supernatural stories of the Cotswolds is that of the ghostly Battle of Edgehill. This is best told in the words of a pamphlet published a year after the battle. It has been given a motif number by E. Baughman in his *Type and Motif-Index of the Folktales of England and North America*, E402.1.8(1). The description (sounds of battle recur at site where it was fought) is inadequate to the visual as well as the auditory appearances described in the pamphlet – but these appear to have faded and grown less vivid. Peter Underwood, investigating the phenomenon, says on the authority of the Rev. John C. Dening that several local people had claimed to hear sounds of the battle in the air on the anniversary of the battle, 23 October. There are similar traditions at Marston Moor, Tewkesbury and Sedgemoor, though nothing so vivid and circumstantial as this:

Edge-Hill, in the very confines of Warwickshire, neere unto
Keynton in Northamptonshire, a place, as appeares by the sequele,
destined for civill warres and battells; as where King John fought
a battell with his Barons, and where, in defence of the King-
domes lawes and libertie, was fought a bloody conflict betweene
his Majesties and the Parliaments forces; at this Edge-Hill, in the
very place where the battell was strucken, have since, and doth
appeare, strange and portentuous Apparitions of two jarring and
contrary Armies, as I shall in order deliver, it being certified by
the men of most credit in those parts, as, William Wood, Esquire,
Samuel Marshall, Minister, and others, on Saturday, which was in
Christmas time, as if the Saviour of the world, who died to redeem
mankinde, had beene angry that so much Christian blood was
there spilt, and so had permitted these infernall Armies to appeare
where the corporeall Armies had shed so much blood; between
twelve and one of the clock in the morning was heard by some
sheepherds, and other countrey-men, and travellers, first the
sound of drummes afar off, and the noyse of souldiers, as it were,
giving out their last groanes; at which they were much amazed,
and amazed stood still, till it seemed, by the neerenesse of the
noyse, to approach them; at which too much affrighted, they
sought to withdraw as fast as possibly they could; but then, on
the sudden, whilest they were in these cogitations, appeared in
the ayre the same incorporeall souldiers that made those clamours,
and immediately, with Ensignes display'd, Drummes beating,
Musquets going off, Cannons discharged, horses neyghing, which
also to these men were visible, the alarum or entrance to this
game of death was strucke up, one Army, which gave the first
charge, having the Kings colours, and the other the Parliaments,
in their head or front of the battells, and so pell mell to it they
went; the battell that appeared to the Kings forces seeming at
first to have the best, but afterwards to be put into apparent rout;
but till two or three in the morning, in equall scale continued
this dreadfull fight, the clattering of Armes, noyse of Cannons,
cries of souldiers, so amazing and terrifying the poore men, that
they could not believe they were mortall, or give credit to their
eares and eyes; runne away they durst not, for feare of being
made a prey to these infernall souldiers, and so they, with much
feare and affright, stayed to behold the successe of the businesse,
which at last suited to this effect: after some three houres fight,
that Army which carryed the Kings colours withdrew, or rather

appeared to flie; the other remaining, as it were, masters of the
field, stayed a good space triumphing, and expressing all the signes
of joy and conquest, and then, with all their Drummes, Trumpets,
Ordnance, and Souldiers, vanished; the poore men glad they were
gone, that had so long staid them there against their wils, made
with all haste to Keinton, and there knocking up Mr Wood, a
Justice of Peace, who called up his neighbour, Mr Marshall, the
Minister, they gave them an acount of the whole passage, and
averred it upon their oaths to be true. At which affirmation of
theirs, being much amazed, they should hardly have given credit
to it, but would have conjectured the men to have been either mad
or drunk, had they not knowne some of them to have been of
approved integritie: and so, suspending their judgements till the
next night about the same houre, they, with the same men, and
all the substantiall Inhabitants of that and the neighbouring
parishes, drew thither; where, about halfe an houre after their
arrivall, on Sunday, being Christmas night, appeared in the same
tumultuous warlike manner, the same two adverse Armies, fighting with as much spite and spleen as formerly: and so departed
the Gentlemen and all the spectatours, much terrified with these
visions of horrour, withdrew themselves to their houses, beseech-
ing God to defend them from those hellish and prodigious
enemies. The next night they appeared not . . . but on the
ensuing Saturday night, in the same place, and at the same
houre, they were again seene with far greater tumult, fighting in
the manner afore-mentioned for foure houres, or verie neere,
and then vanished, appearing againe on Sunday night, and per-
forming the same actions of hostilitie and bloudshed; so that both
Mr Wood and others, whose faith, it should seeme, was not strong
enough to carrie them out against these delusions, forsook their
habitations thereabout, and retired themselves to other more
secure dwellings; but Mr Marshall stayed, and some other; and so
successively the next Saturday and Sunday the same tumult and
prodigious sights and actions were put in the state and condition
they were formerly. The rumour whereof comming to his Majestie
at Oxford, he immediately dispatched thither Colonell Lewis Kirke,
Captaine Dudley, Captaine Wainman, and three other Gentlemen
of credit, to take the full view and notice of the said businesse,
who, first hearing the true attestation and relation of Mr Marshall
and others, staid there till Saturday night following, wherein they
heard and saw the fore-mentioned prodigies, and so on Sunday,

distinctly knowing divers of the apparitions or incorporeall sub-
stances by their faces, as that of Sir Edmund Varney, and others
that were there slaine; of which upon oath they made testimonie
to his Majestie. What this doth portend, God only knoweth, and
time perhaps will discover; but doubtlesly it is a signe of his
wrath against this Land, for these civill wars, which He in his
good time finish, and send a sudden peace between his Majestie
and Parliament.

12 Folk Motifs in Cotswold Churches

WHEN WE TRY TO VISUALISE the interior of the Cotswold churches in the thirteenth, fourteenth and fifteenth centuries we have to call up a picture of great detail and colour, in some ways less beautiful than the long sweeping lines and curves of pale limestone that we can see in well-preserved churches today, where the eye can follow unimpeded the solid pillars and simple arches of the Norman work or the delicate interlacing columns and architraves of the perpendicular, with the lovely texture of the stone showing in every carved head or intricate monster. In medieval times the interior of every church was an illuminated manual by which the illiterate could be taught the elements of the Faith, a gallery of saints on whom individual devotions could be concentrated, and many a *memento mori* with skeletons or half-decayed corpses lying beneath stately monuments. These were the visual aids by which the village priest brought home to an illiterate congregation the lessons that he wished to teach: biblical history, or ethics or devotion. 'Look!' he could say, pointing to the Doom just above him, 'see what kind of things drunkards will have to drink! Look at that cruel man whose flesh is being torn by hooks! Don't you think he wishes he had been more merciful to his neighbours? Look at that naked wanton being carried to Hell-mouth on a devil's back. What comfort is her fine headdress to her now? But see how St Peter welcomes in that good old soul that was so constant with her prayers and her charity. It doesn't matter that in this life she was weak and poor; the saints are greeting her and leading her into Heaven.' And as he pointed from place to place in the church, to bring home one lesson or another, all heads would turn.

But the church served another purpose as well as these. It was a great picture-book, full of stories and jokes and country proverbs. And there was good magic in it too to keep the Devil at bay and to guard men travelling and to make crops and flocks fertile. We look first nowadays at the old glass windows – if any remain – and at the stone carvings but perhaps the first thing to catch the worshipper's eye in old times would be the wall paintings. Most of these have faded, or been covered by successive coats of whitewash, but a few remain almost as brilliant as ever and remnants of others give us an idea of the subjects that were treated in the paintings. The greater number of the churches would have a St Christopher painted on the north wall, directly opposite the south door. St Christopher, as most motorists know, is the patron saint of travellers, and anyone bound on a journey, as perilous in old days as the motorways are now, could turn before he left the church and say a parting prayer to the saint.

His legend is a pure piece of folklore. It is given in the *Legenda Aurea* of Jacques de Voragine. There was once a mighty heathen giant called Reprobus. He was so proud and strong that he determined to serve only the greatest in the world. So he went to the great Pharaoh of Egypt and served him quite happily until he noticed that he always crossed himself when the Devil was mentioned. It was clear that the Devil was stronger than Pharaoh. So Reprobus left Pharaoh and went to look for the Devil. He found him easily enough and began to serve him with all his might. But after a while he found that the Devil, great and strong and proud though he was, could never pass a wayside cross, but had to make a big circuit. It was plain that there was someone stronger than the Devil and after a while Reprobus found out that it was Christ. He knew a hermit near by who was a servant of Christ, so he went to him and asked what he should do to serve Christ, since he could not see him. 'Say your prayers,' said the hermit, but Reprobus did not know how to do that, so the hermit set him an easier task. There was a great river flowing near his cell and the hermit set Reprobus to carry travellers across. With his great strength this was an easy task to him and he went readily out one night when he heard himself called. It was a tiny child that he had to lift but when he had set him on his shoulders he had never felt anything so heavy. But he stepped down with him into the stream, which seemed to grow deeper and stronger, and the wind got up and the weight on his shoulder grew heavier and heavier until he could hardly stand under it. But still he went on, step by step, until he reached the shore; and as he set the child down he said, 'You seemed to me to weigh as heavy as the whole world.' 'You say the truth, Christopher,' said the child. 'I carry the weight of the world and all its sins on my shoulders. I made the world and I saved the world and I carry its sins. And tonight you have carried them for me.' And with that he vanished and Christopher knew that it was the Christ Child that he had carried over the river that night. The story seems obviously intended as an allegory rather than a history, yet relics of St Christopher were everywhere in medieval times and there were quite a number of arms preserved in various churches.

Baunton church has the best preserved of the Christopher murals, with a riverside landscape and two fishermen, one of them catching a fish. There was a large one over the north door in Bloxham church but it has faded a good deal since the last description of it. The kneeling hermit can still be made out but the mermaid who used to live in the river is not easy to find. She would be put there to indicate the stormy weather, for the appearance of a mermaid was supposed to foretell a storm. Traces of Christopher pictures are to be found in Widford church, at Horley and at Souldern. At Heythrop there is a sixteenth-century stained-glass window of St Christopher.

Nearly every church that had pictorial murals would be likely to have a Doom painting at the east end. A most excellent example of this, with all its three parts clear and distinct, is to be found at North Leigh. It is placed as usual over the chancel arch and is in unusually bright, clear colours – the reds for instance a fresh scarlet instead of the red umber more generally used. The three parts are divided by bands of red daisies. In the centre the dead are rising from beautifully carved sepulchres; on the left is Hell – a flaming Hell-mouth with the armed legs of a knight sticking out of it. A hideous devil is beckoning the next victim, a bishop, from a hesitant group. On the right side rise the walls of Heaven, with St Peter welcoming the souls as they arrive. An unusual incident is also introduced: an angel leaning over the wall of Heaven to pull up a soul who is unconventionally scaling it.

Shorthampton, a small church near to Charlbury, has had an unusually fine set of paintings. They were discovered under coats of plaster in 1903 and were refreshed and fully described in 1937. Since then they seem to have faded, though much that was described can still be made out. There was a large and impressive Doom over the chancel arch, with a cauldron full of boiling souls and a large devil tootling a horn. There is a fine Doom also at South Leigh – if that can be counted as in the Cotswolds. There is one at Coombe and at Hook Norton. It is in the treatment of Hell that the folk imagination is let loose. Heaven is generally treated more in accordance with theology.

Other apocryphal and legendary themes are to be found in the wall paintings. Shorthampton is rich in them. The story of St Eligidius or Eloy is one, seen elsewhere in stone carvings but rare in murals. St Eligidius shared with St Clement the office of patron of blacksmiths. Before he became a churchman he had been a smith. Once a carter brought an old horse to him, so frantic with pain that no smith could handle him. St Eloy cut off the leg, carried it to the fire and shod it, and then returned it to the horse. In this picture the horse is being supported in a wooden frame while St Eloy hammers away at the forge. Another unusual picture illustrates an episode from the Apocryphal *Gospel of Nicodemus*. It is the story of how Christ as a boy made little clay birds and brought them to life to entertain his play-fellows. We can just make out Christ sitting at the Virgin's knee with a bird in his hand and a companion below him holding up his hands in amazement. This little church, counted now as part of the parish of Charlbury, will fall into disrepair unless it is soon attended to.

The old church at Oddington has one of the finest Dooms in the countryside, a large and well-restored thirteenth-century painting. Christ Himself is receiving the saved at the entrance to Paradise, near Hell-mouth a figure is hanging on a gallows and a woman is in a pillory. More difficult to discern, a palimpsest near shows a piece of popular satire, a fox preaching in a monk's habit. The church stands apart from the village, which was moved to clearer air at the time of the Plague.

These little chuches, too humble for elaborate carvings, generally made up for the lack of them by wall paintings. St Oswald's little church, between Swinbrook and Burford, is an example of this. It is on the site of a Roman villa; every grave in the small churchyard was dug through a Roman pavement, part of which is to be seen in the church. I have already mentioned the remains of the St Christopher mural on the north wall, partly obscured by a painting of the royal arms but a rarer and even more legendary story is that of the three young and lusty kings hunting in the forests who were met by three crowned skeletons. More perfect illustrations of this subject are to be found in other parts of Oxfordshire but the close proximity of Wychwood, the hunting place of kings, must have made this story specially appropriate. Many other churches, among them Ampney Crucis and Ampney St Mary, have wall paintings but many of them are palimpsests and, with paintings one on top of another, are very difficult to decipher. Many of them also must have been completely destroyed, as, for instance, the Whitsuntide procession in Cirencester described by Rudder, but now quite invisible.

Carvings in wood or stone are even richer in folk motifs than the wall-paintings and many of them are tucked away in obscure places as if the craftsmen had not been quite sure of ecclesiastical approval. The gargoyles that cover the water-spouts on the outside of the churches are generally hideous and grotesque creatures, apparently demons, but their purpose was to frighten away the Devil and evil spirits. The weather-cock, the Church Grim, who appears to have been the ghost of the foundation sacrifice, and the gargoyles were the three protectors of the church against evil influences, according to folk beliefs. But the heads most definitely connected with folk practices were those of the Green Men. These occur in a great many of the Cotswold churches – and indeed all over England. They merit and are now receiving very special study. In a conference held on 'Symbols of Power' at Lancaster University in April of 1973 Mrs Kathleen Basford read a remarkable paper, 'The Quest for the Green Man', illustrated with photographs of very high quality. The paper will be published with the other transactions of the conference but it is to be hoped that Mrs Basford will produce a full-length book on the subject. There seem to be at least two, possibly three, different types of Green Man to be seen in church carvings: a man dressed and covered in greenery like the Jack-in-the-Green who took part in the fertility rituals of the spring games and then a more potent and sinister figure with a protruding tongue who appears to be sprouting greenery from his mouth and sometimes his nostrils and eyes. It has been suggested that this represents a victim sacrificed by strangling as a fertility rite, a kind of John Barleycorn. This is the form in which the Green Man most commonly appears in churches but occasionally there are heads whose hair and beards are sprouting leaves and these seem most likely to be wood spirits or gods without human origins.

The second type is the commonest in churches but inn signs most frequently exhibit the Jack-in-the-Green. It is curious that one of the three carved stones, still kept in the new Banbury church and brought from the beautiful old one so wantonly destroyed in the eighteenth century, is a Green Man. Adderbury, which is rich in so many stone carvings, has half a dozen Green Men carved in wood on its remarkable choir stalls and nodding seats. Some are of the hanged-man type, with protruding tongues, and some more like wood spirits, with hair and beards of foliage. It has besides two fine stone ones. Stanton has a Green Man with a protruding tongue. Great Rollright has a man with an oak leaf in his mouth and a woman with a branch of acorns. Many more are to be found by careful search. Often they are set so high that it is difficult to see them without field glasses or telescopic lenses.

Strange beasts are even more common, particularly dragons and worms. Adderbury is rich in monsters as well as in country scenes. More than a hundred figures are to be found round the exterior of the tower and under the parapet of both aisles. On the south side there is a magnificent dragon with a knotted tail and a fine gryphon and on the north a dragon with one head and two bodies, a man drawing his sword to fight a loathly worm on his back, a two-tailed mermaid, an archer who has aimed at a monster and hit an old woman instead, and a wonderful procession of folk musicians playing pan-pipes, cymbals, a hurdy-gurdy, bagpipes, a fiddle and a harp. Inside on the corbels of the roof are some country scenes, a woman blowing up a fire with bellows and a shepherd with his sheep. At Bloxham, which lies not far from Adderbury, is another procession of musicians, set so high up where the tower meets the spire that it is not easy to study them in detail, but they are full of lively movement. This is on the north side of the tower but round the corner to the south is a scene of even greater interest, the illustration of a nursery rhyme:

John, John, John!
The grey goose is gone!
And the fox is away to his den oh.

The fox is escaping with the goose, the man is chasing him with a stick and the old woman is shaking her distaff.

Alkerton, six miles west of Banbury, seems to share the same tradition of carvings as we find in Adderbury, Bloxham and Wroxton, though in Wroxton the style is more Flemish and the figures are on the whole naturalistic except for a fine gryphon on the chancel screen. The Alkerton carvings are supposed to celebrate the life of the Black Prince, though there are musicians, one playing an organ and another a harp, and a muzzled bear.

Hanwell is another church not far from Banbury which has a fine array of carvings, among them a mermaid. Hook Norton has a centaur, Saggitarius, the zodiacal sign, and a two-headed monster whose heads are fighting together. It is suggested that this symbolises the self-destructive power of evil. There is also a figure which might signify an elf – a tiny man peering through the beard of another.

The fine carving of Lower Swell may be more intellectualised and symbolic than that in some of the other churches. On the tympanum of the south porch is a carving of the Tree of Life with a dove eating its fruits and over the chancel arch is a series of carvings said to represent the life of man and the mastery given him over the beasts. There is a serpent, a hare, a seated man, a bird hanging from a bough, a stag, a dog, a cat, a lion. This may represent the naming of the creatures by Adam. There are three interlaced rings, a standing man and three fishes, said to represent baptism.

Among the fine carvings of Northleach are angel musicians and demon heads and one of the grotesques supporting the pedestals is of a cat playing a fiddle to three rats.

As we go towards Cirencester we see many fine churches. Among them North Cerney is rich in carvings of fantastic creatures. On the south transept there are some manticoras – creatures with the bodies of lions and the heads of men. Some of these are even more grotesque than the manticoras of the bestiaries. One has the head and arms of a man, the body and legs of a dog – but with hoofs – and a tail like a beaver's. Another has the head of a man, the body of a leopard, a long tail 'coward' – that is passing between its legs and curled upward – and, again, hoofs. The carvings at South Cerney are equally fine.

Southrop has a remarkable font on which are carved the virtues trampling down the vices and the horned figure of Moses acknowledging Ecclesia and repudiating the discarded and blinded figure of Synagoga. These are only samples of the carvings to be found in Cotswold churches.

Stained glass shows fewer folk motifs than the carvings, partly because so many of the windows were destroyed at the Reformation or during the Civil War, but mainly because most of the windows were devoted to more orthodox themes. Fairford's glorious Doom window and the devils set above the persecutors in the north clerestory windows are an exception but, Fairford is generally excluded from the Cotswold area – even by people who describe Cirencester as the capital of the Cotswolds.

Perhaps the stained glass most interesting to the folklorist is not to be found in a church but in Buckland Rectory. This is the oldest rectory to be continuously inhabited in England. It consists of three parts: a half-timbered medieval house, a hall that was used by the abbot of Hailes as a judicial hall, and a later building connected with it. The three parts form a kind of squat H. The windows in the abbot's hall are filled with fifteenth-century painted glass. The design is a formal one, representing the courting dance of the blackcock. Blackcock and hares have in common an elaborate courting dance and were both deeply suspected of being witches in consequence. The blackcock were common enough in the Cotswolds in early times but were persecuted as witches. Hares managed to survive but the blackcock disappeared out of England and are now only slowly beginning to return where conditions are favourable to them. The blackcock in these windows, painted in black and yellow on plain glass, are in the characteristic positions of their courting dance but bear in their bills a scroll, *In nomine Jesu* to hallow their activities. Some of them are transfixed with arrows like Cock Robin in the nursery rhyme. It is possible that Cock Robin was not a redbreast at all, but the witch's Robinet – or familiar – but this is merely a matter of surmise. Buckland church has a fine piece of fifteenth-century glass in its east window. It originally represented the seven sacraments; baptism, marriage and extreme unction are those that remain. The great treasure of the church is the famous Buckland Bowl which is made of maple wood with a silver rim and a silver disc in the base engraved with a figure of St Margaret holding a book and treading upon her dragon. It was once the loving cup used at village weddings and is a very unusual survival of an ancient custom.

The beautiful monumental tombs to be found in an uncounted number of Cotswold churches belong rather to history than to folklore but traditions have grown up around some of the monuments. In the Wilcote Chapel at North Leigh church there are fifteenth-century effigies of Sir William and Lady Wilcote – or possibly of Lady Wilcote and her second husband, John Blackett. Angelina Parker, writing in 1923 in Volume xxxiv of *Folklore,* records how an old woman told her that as children they had observed that Lady Wilcote's praying hands did not quite touch. They were persuaded that they were gradually parting and that when they had grown apart she would get up and haunt the place. There was a legend that treasure had been discovered by some workmen under the tomb. They had taken it away but such disturbances had arisen in the church that they had been forced to return it. The old woman used often to visit the church rather nervously to see if Lady Wilcote's hands were any further apart. Actually the husband's hands are the further apart now, so perhaps he is the most likely to walk. It is possible that Lady Wilcote had the reputation of a formidable woman and that that reputation survived for 400 years as Lady Tanfield's has done. Even in the 1950s a workman cleaning the Tanfield memorial in Burford church did not care to work alone in the Tanfield Chapel.

A historical tradition clings to the tomb of Sir Edmund Bray, the seventeenth-century owner of Shipton Court. His effigy in the church at Shipton-under-Wychwood shows the sword at his right side instead of his left. It is said that it was his misfortune to kill a man by a hasty blow in a quarrel and he vowed never again to use his right hand.

Some of the churches have Roman pagan altars built into them and in one church at least this has given rise to a curious legend. In Bisley, on a side road between Chalford and Stroud, there is a field called Church Piece and the legend arose that the church originally stood there and was supernaturally carried to its present site. This is a widespread legend, Type ML 7060. There seems to have been some vagueness in this case about who the transporter was: the Devil, a saint or a supernatural animal. The legend differs in different places and in Bisley it seems to have slipped out of the common memory. The curious thing is that when the church was restored in 1862 a Roman altar was discovered with the figure of a horseman on it, which seems to have been carried from its original position in Church Piece, where there are considerable Roman

L

remains. It was unfortunately removed to the British Museum. Since its existence was not known until 1862 this seems an example of folk memory with its curious power of retention and distortion.

A further study of the Cotswold churches would no doubt uncover a great quantity of folk practices and beliefs which have left a mark in them.

13 Trades and Crafts in the Cotswolds

STONE AND WOOL dominated the Cotswolds from early times, though there were other crafts as well that played their part in men's lives. I have already mentioned the wide area to which the Cotswold stone penetrated and the use of the quarries from Roman times onwards. The methods of working were equally traditional. Some 15 or more years ago the workmen repairing Sudeley Castle used tools and methods of working that had descended without alteration from Norman times. A little earlier a Burford neighbour who was architect of her own house found a stone mason to make her a fire-place with tools whose design dated back to the Norman Conquest. There were various branches of the stone trade: the quarrying and shaping, the masonry work and finally the carving, very individual and often local. The churchyards and church tombs are generally peculiar in style to one place or area. In Taynton, for instance, there appears to have been a traditional design of flat scroll-work which appears on the Sylvester tombs in Burford Lady Chapel, on the Harmon tomb and on most of the tombs in Taynton church. The design resembles the cartouche of a seventeenth-century book. The banker masons, who do fine finishing work such as lintels and fire-places and even carvings, are the highest grade of the working stone-masons. In the past they will have been responsible for some of the church carvings noted in the last chapter. Some will have been the work of visiting artists but many of special folklore interest seem to have been local in inception. It is to be remarked that a cluster of churches – Hanwell, Adderbury, Wroxton and others – have carvings of musicians and of fabulous monsters unlike those found in any other part of the Cotswolds.

The quarrymen formed local communities and must have shared a communal life each with its own traditions but these have now died out with the workings. There is no trace of any mine spirits – such as haunted the Cornish mines – probably because most of the quarrying was open and only in Taynton and Stonesfield were there extensive underground workings.

The initiation ceremonies seem also to have perished. One custom that still survives in the building trade is that of 'capping'. When the masonry work is finished and the chimneys are put on, a flag is run up from one chimney and everyone downs tools and gathers round for a drink. A master builder suggests that the flag was originally run up to summon the farm hands and other voluntary labourers to help in lifting the heavy roof-tree to the ridge. They would naturally be inspirited by a drink

The great church buildings of the Cotswolds brought subsidiaries of the masonic works in stone carving and indirectly in wood-carving, for which Burford was once famous. The stained glass was often imported, like that of Fairford.

The wool trade, however, had many more subsidiary industries attached to it, with their attendant mysteries. The shepherd's calling dates from the earliest civilisations. From early times the profession of shepherd was morally ambivalent. On the one hand they repre-sented pastoral innocence – it will be remembered that the innocent Abel was a herdsman and Cain a tiller of the soil. The shepherds of classical literature lived a life of innocence devoted to the service of Pan and in Christian tradition the place of the shepherds in the nativity hallows them. In the medieval miracle play, however, the character of Mack the sheep-stealer shows a realistic appreciation of the temptations to which a shepherd was exposed and this aspect of the shepherd's character is amply represented in the Cotswold tradition of murderous gangs of sheep-stealers. In Germany and some of the other mid-European countries the shepherd belonged to one of the 'black trades' because of his infrequent attendance at Mass. A trace of this is to be found in the Cotswold custom of burying a shepherd with a wisp of wool in his hand, to excuse his frequent enforced absence from church. The shepherd's great days were the sheep-shearing feasts and the lamb feasts.

Hurdle-making may be classed as a subsidiary to the shepherd's mystery. This was a craft often hereditary in a family. Until very recently there was a hurdle-maker with several generations behind him at Fifield, on the wold between Burford and Stow.

From Norman days until the fifteenth century great bales of raw wool were shipped overseas to the wool-staple towns. The lime-grown grass of the uplands was suitable for grazing and the great sheep of the Cotswolds, 'the Cotswold lions' as they were called, produced long weighty fleeces. The Flemish traders came over as early as the twelfth century to buy fleeces from all over England. A story from a chronicle of that period cited by H. A. Evans illustrates the period before the export trade was set up and the wool-staple towns appointed : the time in which visiting merchants rode round the countryside collecting their bales of wool. In 1114 some canons of Laon crossed over to England to collect subscriptions for the rebuilding of their church. They were joined on the boat by a party of Flemish merchants going to buy wool, with money bags which contained more than 300 marks of silver. During the passage a pirate ship came in sight and began speedily to overhaul them. The merchants were terrified and ran to the altar of Our Lady, casting all their money bags upon it and vowing that if only the Virgin would free them from the danger of the pirates she should have all their money for the rebuilding of her church. At once a wind sprang up and the ship made away from the pirates and got safe into port. The canons were sorry for the merchants and intended to give them a little out of their dedicated bags so that they should not land penniless in England but the merchants did not wait for their charity. Each man picked up his bag again and, after a fervent verbal tribute to the Virgin, carried it on shore and left the canons amazed. But Providence caught up with them. They travelled all over England and carried great bales of wool down to Dover where they stowed it in a barn while they bargained for a ship. But in the night a great thunderstorm arose, the barn was struck and every bundle of wool burned to ashes. So the merchants learned that they could not play fast and loose with the Queen of Heaven.

By the thirteenth century the one parish of Beverstone alone grazed nearly 6,000 sheep. In the fourteenth century seven of the great monastic houses of Gloucestershire were sending weighty consignments of wool to Flanders and Italy. Then the great merchants began to arise: the Cely family who collected their wool mainly in Northleach and William Grevel of Chipping Campden, who was called the flower of the wool merchants of all England. He died in 1401.

This was wholesale trade on both national and international levels but it touched the individual small farmer, for the merchant trader rode all over the upland country with his 14lbs of tested weights at his saddle-bow, as I described in an earlier chapter. The wool flowed from the shepherd to the European market as surely as a mountain brook flows into a river and the river to the sea. There was specialisation and wholesale trading in weaving as well as with the raw wool but perhaps the links with the cottage crafts were closer in weaving than in the export of fleeces. It certainly seems to have come earlier, even from Roman times for it used to be believed that Chedworth Manor housed a dyeing and fulling industry at the end of the Roman occupation. Doubt is now thrown on this, though the presence of meadow saffron among the local wild flowers and of a fine deposit of fuller's earth makes the conjecture plausible. At any rate spindle-whorls have been excavated there and in other Romano-British encampments. A Saxon weaver's hut was recently found near the Windrush at Bourton-on-the-Water. Woollen mills were set up first in areas just below the Cotswolds, though the wool came from the upland sheep, but later they moved up into the Stroud and Painswick area.

Spinning was for long a cottage industry, and there were many cottage looms. In the sixteenth century fine broadcloth began to be made and for that wool had to be imported, for the Cotswold wool was too long and stringy. Witney was a very early weaving town and by the seventeenth century had begun to specialise in blankets. Robert Plot in 1705 gives a full and careful account of the Witney blanket manufacture in his time. All the main Cotswold towns practised weaving from the fifteenth to the seventeenth centuries – Cirencester, Chipping Campden, Northleach, Banbury, Burford, Charlbury, Stroud, Painswick, Randwick and many others.

Randwick is particularly notable because of its 'wap' with the weaver's song which marks it as the celebration of a weaving community. Charlbury was the centre of a cottage weaving industry, the cloth being collected from the neighbouring villages. Different towns began to specialise in different types of weaving, as for instance the narrow-braid looms of Burford, a work to which Burford children were apprenticed through the eighteenth century as well as to the broad-weaving. In the sixteenth century Banbury was famous for its 'blue-bonnets', a beret-like kind of cap, but the Banbury horse market led to specialisation in webbing and horse-cloths in the seventeenth century. In the eighteenth century Banbury and the area round manufactured a great quantity of woollen plush, which went all over Europe for royal liveries and supplied covers to the seating of the Houses of Parliament. When Banbury moved over to the manufacture of machinery the little neighbouring village of Shutford still supplied plush for the Royal Foresters of Windsor, for the House of Commons, for Germany, Spain and the Shah of Persia.

According to Christine Sibbit the industry closed down in 1948. E. C. Williams, in the 1951 edition of her *Companion into Oxfordshire*, gives a lively account of her visit to two of the last four of the hand-loom workers. There was still a small factory in Shutford and a few power-loom workers in the houses. Miss Williams was conducted by an old lady of 82, who still scrutinised each piece of plush woven in the factory and replaced faulty threads by hand. The old hand-weavers were great artists in their craft and proud to display it but the trade had fallen on hard times: since the war Germany no longer needed the golden plush used for the royal uniforms, Republican Spain ordered no more of the gorgeous scarlet used by the royal guards and the new Shah of Persia had cancelled the order for purple plush.

The neighbourhood of Cirencester is more fortunate in a demand for its broadcloth for hunting pink and the cardinal's purple, though the demand for footman's liveries has sunk almost to nothing. In the Festival of Britain year in 1951 Cirencester mounted a magnificent display of broadcloth with giant straw figures, wearing purple, scarlet and black, displaying two Cotswold crafts at the same time, for the straw modelling was formerly practised there too.

There were many subsidiaries to the wool trade. In Witney, where the blankets were originally woven of wool clipped from the pelts, pelt-mongering held at first an equal place with blanket-making.

The skins were sold to Bampton to be made up into coats, waistcoats and breeches. Burford was famous – Plot says 'from time immemorial' – for its saddles. In the seventeenth century they were thought to be the best in Europe.

Glove-making, from sheep skins and-deer skins, was practised in Woodstock, Witney and Burford, also in Charlbury. Both women and men worked at the craft but the women outnumbered the men by three to one. There were glove factories where the gloves were cut and sent out to the cottages and this pattern is still maintained. Mrs Falconer's story of the phantom coach in Chapter 6 illustrates the way in which the work was distributed. The apprentice glovers, who worked in factories or under a master, were admitted to full status by an initiation ceremony, as in other mysteries.

Smithies are now difficult to find and in great demand but formerly there was one in every considerable village and a small town like Burford had three. Much folk tradition attached to the smiths, for they were believed to have some occult knowledge: iron was sovereign against witchcraft and smiths were supposed to have special knowledge about forging particularly potent horseshoes and nails. The smiths had a double craft: they were generally expert farriers and many of them were skilled workers in wrought-iron. The Filkins Folk Museum is rich in specimens of the village smith's art, among them a highwayman's horse-shoe, an ingenious little gadget for grilling a herring, shoes for the oxen who ploughed the land instead of horses and a tool to make nuts and bolts. The thread of the screw would be peculiar to that particular blacksmith. This makes one realise how local these crafts were. (It will be remembered that a smith recognised that Charles 11 was a fugitive from Worcester because his horse had been shod in three different counties.)

In the same way the different sizes of roofing slates have special and different names in each area. Sometimes the tilers are reluctant to give the names for their slates, regarding them as part of their mystery. There is, however, a list of one set of tiles in Burford Museum, containing such picturesque names as Muffetties and Long Wyvetts.

What might be called a subsidiary of the blacksmith's work was the Woodstock steel – highly ornate ornaments made of blacksmith's nails. This craft was started as early as the sixteenth century and was in high demand in Paris in the eighteenth. Chains, buttons, buckles, seals, snuffers, scissors and sword hilts were made in studded patterns and highly polished. At the end of the eighteenth century a small pair of scissors cost 18 guineas in Woodstock and a 2oz chain was sold for £170 in Paris in 1813.

Several of the small towns had rope walks in them. In Burford the rope was spun straight across the main street in the nineteenth century. The Hill was only a rough track in those days, for the main traffic went along Witney Street, across High Street and out by Sheep Street. There were many small home trades, such as basket-making and rush-mat making, practised in the villages.

Some places had individual industries. Boddicote near Banbury, for instance, specialised for some hundreds of years in the growing of herbs and Winchcombe in tobacco. They made a great profit from it, for the climate and soil were more suitable for tobacco than for the growth of corn. The monopolies which were a feature of James I's government, forbade it, but still the culture continued. After the destruction of Winchcombe Abbey the town had fallen into great poverty and the culture of tobacco provided profitable employment for the 4,000 beggars noted in 1649. Virginia's interests were made paramount, however, and the parliament of Charles II forbade the growth of tobacco in England. The people of Winchcombe and other tobacco-growers defied the prohibition. Edith Brill quotes the account given by the *Mercurius Politicus* of July 1658. The Life Guards were sent to Winchcombe as Samuel Pepys recorded, to spoil the fields of tobacco and dig up the plants but, as the *Mercurius Politicus* said: 'the country did rise against them in a great body, giving them reviling and threatening speeches, even to kill them, horse and men . . . insomuch, the tumult being so great, he was constrained to draw off and nothing more was done.' However in the end the government won and the tobacco-growers had recourse to pamphleteering and brought out ' Henry Hangman's Horror, or Gloucestershire's Request to the Smokers and Tobacco-nists of London' in which Henry Hangman complains of the decline of his trade since the planting of tobacco, ' especially at Winch-combe, before tobacco was planted, there being no kind of trade to employ men necessity compelled poor men to stand my friend, by stealing of sheep and other cattel, breaking of hedges robbing of orchards and what not.' Even this plea was disregarded, and in the end Winchcombe had to give up its tobacco and sink back into destitution.

Local foods, especially those eaten at festivals, have been men-tioned from time to time in this book. Banbury cakes and Banbury

cheese were some of the most famous. The Banbury cake as we know
it now is a boat-shaped, flaky pastry crust containing a rich fruit
filling but something rather different is suggested by the sixteenth-
century description of 'bagge puddings or panne puddings made
with flower, frittars, pancakes such as we call Banberrie cakes'.
Banbury cheese was considered a great delicacy. It was sold all over
England and sent abroad in the fifteenth century as a royal gift.
In 1756 the sale was still considerable but by 1841 the very memory
of how to make it had vanished. A recipe from the reign of Henry
VIII survives in a Bodleian manuscript, Sloane 1201, but it is even
vaguer than most of the early recipes and it would be a bold man
who tried to make cheese from it.

'To make Banberry chese' it runs:

Take a thin ches fat And hote mylk, as it comes from the cows
And Ryn it forth wtal in Somertyme, And kned your couddes bot
ones. And kned them not to smal bot brake them ones with your
handes And in Somer tyme salt the Couddes nothyng bot let the
chese lye iij dayes unsalted and then salt them. And lay oon upon
an other but not to much salt. And so shall they gether butter And
in Wynter tyme in lyke Wyse bot then hote your mylk And salt
your Couddes for then it will gether butter of it self. Take the
Wrung Whey of the same mylk and let it stand a day or ij till
it have a Creme, and it shal make as good butter as any other.

The foundation of Huntley & Palmer's biscuit manufacturing
at Reading was laid in Burford at the beginning of the nineteenth
century. A Mr Huntley started a small private school for boys at the
top of the Hill, not far from the present Roman Catholic church.
His wife catered for the pupils. She was an excellent cook and
among other things she made some biscuits which were so popular
that she started a small bakery for them near the mill in Witney
Street. This flourished, and in the end a Mr Palmer joined in partnership with Mrs Huntley and set up a factory in Reading. It is to be
supposed that Mr Huntley gave up his school and followed his wife's
fortunes. At least such is the tradition.

In consequence of a number of charitable bequests for the
apprenticing of poor children, the Burford parish council possesses
a collection of indentures from the end of the seventeenth to the
mid-nineteenth century. The eighteenth-century collection consists
of 90 indentures. Of these, 37 were apprenticed in Burford, 11 in

Witney, 6 in London and the rest scattered among the neighbouring villages. This is not of course a complete list of the apprentices of the period; it only contains the children considered poor enough to qualify for a premium paid by charity, but the list of the trades represented gives one a picture of the general set-up of a country town in the eighteenth-century Cotswolds. They comprise broad-weavers, victualler, shoemaker, barber and periwig makers, wor-cested weaver, narrow weavers, innholder, carpenter, cordwainers, blacksmith, labourer, tailors' hempdresser and ropemaker, wheel-wright and ploughmaker, yeoman, flaxdresser. Some trades are not represented – which we know to have existed in Burford at that time – as clockmaker, saddler, builder, stonemason, but these would be trades for the wealthier apprentices. Some closely neighbouring villages, such as Fulbrook, Swinbrook and Taynton had tailors and mantua-makers. The whole gives a picture of a bustling little town, with plenty going on and in contact with the rest of the world. The indentures themselves, with their variations, repay study and admit us into the everyday life of our ancestors. Much more remains to be done on the traditions of the trades, the superstitions, the good-and bad-luck beliefs, the initiation ceremonies and anecdotes of notable characters, with traditions of hazards and perils. Much should be collected at once. Much has already gone beyond recording. But the outline of what trades and crafts were practised will give us some idea of the daily life of our predecessors and perhaps make a skeleton which can be clothed by fuller researches.

Notes

1 *General Survey of the Cotswolds*, pages 11–17.

As a preliminary to writing a book on the Cotswolds it is necessary to decide on the area they cover and I found a general disagreement on this. The Curator and Assistant Curator of the Bodleian Library Map Room were most helpful about finding Ordnance Survey maps which covered the area, and their final advice to me was to count any place a part of the Cotswolds which was claimed as such by its inhabitants. The local opinion sometimes seems to make nothing of physical configuration but I have followed this advice in including Long Compton in the Cotswolds, though to the stranger it would seem well at the bottom of the escarpment. For the geographical and geological account of the Cotswolds I have relied on the Victoria County History : *Oxfordshire*, Vol. 1 and *Gloucestershire*, Vol. 1, on Jacquetta Hawkes' geographical, historical and ecological essay *A Land* and on Robert Plot's *Natural History of Oxfordshire*, and for the antiquities on Camden's *Britannia* and R. G Collingwood's *Roman Britain*, 1934, and O. G. S. Crawford's *Long Barrows of the Cotswolds*, 1925. Samuel Rudder's *New History of Gloucestershire*, 1779, is still a standard work, supplementing and bringing up to date Robert Atkyns' *Ancient and Present State of Gloucestershire*, 1712. Besides these there are interesting pieces of information to be found in the standard guide books, unfortunately many of them given without ascription. Methuen's ' Little Guides ' give full and accurate information about the churches, though they are not otherwise very informative. Every village is, however, mentioned in alphabetical order. Macmillan's Highways and Byways series, particularly H. A. Evans' *Oxfordshire and the Cotswolds* is full of tantalising pieces of information but unfortunately without ascription. The County Books series published by Robert Hale have also some very interesting passages and have at least a list of books consulted. The same may be said of E. C. Williams' *Companion into Oxfordshire* which has a classified book list. All these make interesting starting points for exploration, though they naturally contain more topography than folklore. Arthur Mee's King's England series is of something the same standard, with some very pleasing photographic illustrations. Useful field books are *Discovering Gloucestershire and the Cotswolds* and *Discovering Oxfordshire*. The chief references for the Rollright Stones and their legends are given in the text.

The Romance of King Orfeo is to be found in W. C. Hazlitt's *Fairy Tales, Legends and Romances Illustrating Shakespeare*, 1875.

The information about the mosaic workers of Cirencester was given in a lecture on the Roman villa at Woodchester, whose mosaic pavement is uncovered and exhibited once in ten years. The last occasion was in August 1973.

H. D. Traill's *Social England*, Vol. II, gives much information about the early wool trade between pages 139 and 561. The merchant's weight and a note on the method of selling and weighing the wool were shown in a special wool-trade exhibition at the Tolsey Museum in Burford.

Full information about Taynton quarries and other Oxfordshire stone is to be found in that storehouse of information, *Oxford Stone* by W. J. Arkell. The Taynton chapter is pages 54–67. Many references will be made in the course of the book to George Swinford's Folk Museum at Filkins. It is not always open but arrangements for visiting it can always be made.

2 *Seasonal Customs and Festivities*, pages 18–41.

The quotation from Gervase Markham, a voluminous seventeenth-century writer on farming and husbandry, is from *The English Husbandman*, 1612, Part 1, Chapter 5.

THE CANDLEMAS DAY RHYME : *Annual Record of the Oxfordshire and District Folklore Society* for 1950, 10.

MINCHINHAMPTON DIFFERENT : Wright and Lones' *British Calendar Customs*, II, 198.

ST VALENTINE'S DAY : *A.R. of O. & D.F.S.*, 10, already cited.

SHROVETIDE CUSTOMS : Pancake bell rung in Burford and Dursley, Wright and Lones' *British Calendar Customs*, I, 15.

MOTHERING SUNDAY : Wright and Lones' *British Calendar Customs*, I, 15, 47, 49. See also the notes on Calendar Customs, *O. & D.F.S.*, 1950, cited above.

HOLY SATURDAYS : See *A.R. of O. & D.F.S.*, 1955, 14. They quote Aubrey, Ms Lansdowne 231, Wiltshire.

MINCHINHAMPTON THREAD-THE-NEEDLE : Hartland, *Gloucestershire Folklore* quoting *Gloucestershire Notes and Queries*, I, 1881, 453.

RANDWICK WAP : Hartland's *Folklore of Gloucestershire*, 35, quoting *Gloucestershire Notes and Queries*, IV, 1890, 142–4. See Appendix for programme of the modern version.

HOCK MONDAY : Robert Plot, *Natural History of Oxfordshire*, 205–6.

STOBBALL : Hartland's *Gloucestershire* quoting *Gloucestershire Notes and Queries*, II, 1884, 373.

'THE BLACK ARMY' : Wright and Lones' *British Calendar Customs*, II, 159.

Stubbes in his *Anatomie of Abuses*, 1585, 171–2 gives such a lively description of May Games as to make them irresistibly attractive.

THE MAYPOLE SONG : To be found in Hartland's *Folklore of Glouces-tershire*, 18, it is quoted from *Aunt Judy's Magazine*, 1874.

MAY DAY : Flora Thompson, *Lark Rise*, Chapter XIII, 196–204.

Percy Manning, 'Some Oxfordshire Seasonal Festivities', *Folklore*, VIII, 1897, 307 *seq.*

LEGEND OF PUDDEN PIES : Is included in an article by Christina Hole, p. 15, *A.R. of O. & D.F.S.*, 1955.

CHRISTMAS HEMP-SOWING : See the Appendix for one that was sup-posed to have fatal results.

THE PRIVILEGE OF HUNTING IN WYCHWOOD : *The History of Burford*, W. J. Monk, Burford, 1891, 20.

Camden's *Britannia* translated by E. Gibson, 1695, 267.

THE WHITSUN PROCESSION : Rudder, *A New History of Gloucester-shire*, 1779, 23–4 and 361. In this last description he says the figures are in high relief.

ROBIN HOOD PLAY : *British Calendar Customs*, III, 5.

MIDSUMMER FAIR : *The History of Burford*, Monk, 11.

3 *Songs, Dances, Games and Rhymes*, pages 42–55.

'GOOD COMPANY' : The words of this song are given in Alfred Williams' *Folk-Songs of the Upper Thames*, 41.

'GEORGE RIDLER'S OVEN' : The words of this are given by Alfred Williams on 291 but the meaning of the song is examined by R. Nettel in *Sing a Song of England*, 107–9.

BACCA PIPES : This dance was described by Angelina Parker in 'Oxford-shire Village Folklore II', *Folklore* XXXIV, 1923, 332. 'Two Church-warden Pipes placed across each other on the ground, and the performer danced a horn-pipe in and between them. This was not easy in thick, hob-nailed boots, particularly as he whistled his own tune.' The long clay churchwarden pipes were made in several places in the district, among them Filkins.

OLD SPORTS AT FILKINS : *The Annual Report of the Oxford and District Folklore Society*, 1950, 8–9.

SINGING GAMES : Flora Thompson, *Lark Rise*, 134–47.

BLOXHAM DOGS : 'Parish Reputations Preserved in Rhyme, Nickname and Tradition', *A.R. of O. & D.F.S.*, 1953, 10.

FORDHAM SHAGS : Flora Thompson, *Lark Rise*, 202 E. Ettlinger in the 1955 number of *A.R. of O. & D.F.S.*, 8, says that Flora Thompson's 'Fordlow' represented Cottesford. She had been in correspondence with Flora Thompson.

ANALYSIS OF THE 'RIDE A COCK HORSE' RHYME : *The Oxford Diction-ary of Nursery Rhymes*, Iona and Peter Opie, 65–7.

DEMOLITION OF BANBURY CHURCH : May be read in detail in Beesley's

History of Banbury, 532–8, and more briefly in Evans' *Highways and Byways of Oxford and the Cotswolds*.

DRUNKEN DEDDINGTON : In J. M. Falkner's *History of Oxfordshire* Deddington is made part of a quatrain :

> Aynho on the Hill,
> Clifton in the Clay,
> Drunken Deddington,
> And Hempton High-way.

4 *Historical Traditions*, pages 56–68.

Nennius, writing in somewhere about the eighth century, is the first historian to claim that Brut, the grandson of Priam, was the first colonist of Britain. This was much amplified by Geoffrey of Monmouth, who claimed that his history was the translation of an ancient Welsh manuscript given him by his friend Walter Mapes. Gildas, Bede and Orosius do not include the story of Brut in their histories. For particulars and notes see *Six English Chronicles*, edited by J. A. Giles, Bohn Library, 1848.

MAZE AT DOVER GAMES : John Aubrey, *The Remaines of Gentilisme*, 1687, 21.

TAKING OF CIRENCESTER BY A FLIGHT OF SPARROWS : Baddeley's *History of Cirencester* in an introductory note 1–7.

CHAPEL OF EASE AT POSTLIP : H. A. Evans, *Highways and Byways of Oxford and the Cotswolds*, 243.

ROYAL EARLS : Chapter XVI, Baddeley's *History of Cirencester*, 185–97.

COBERLEY'S CLAIM TO DICK WHITTINGTON : Evans' *Highways and Byways of Oxford and the Cotswolds*, 260; see also the *Dictionary of National Biography*.

FRANCIS, LORD LOVEL : *Companion into Oxfordshire* by E. C. Williams, 206–9.

SIR ANTHONY KINGSTON : Evans' *Highways and Byways of Oxfordshire and the Cotswolds*, 317–20.

The quotation from Holinshed is in the second edition of 1587, III, 1006–7.

Laurie Lee, *Cider with Rosie*, 39.

THE BOY OF BISLEY : The leaflet on St Mary's Church, Bisley gives a brief account of Thomas Keble's invention of The Boy of Bisley.

There is a good account of Ditchley and of Sir Henry Lee in E. C. Williams' *Companion into Oxfordshire*, 48–51.

Two of the Memorats of the Battle of Edgehill are derived from *Rambles on the Edgehills* by the Vicar of Radway. The third is to be found in Beesley's *History of Banbury*, 322 and was given by an old labourer of 82. It was remarkably accurate.

Plot's *Account of the Just Devil of Woodstock* is to be found on 210–14.

WOMEN OF ASCOTT : In Mrs Groves' *History of Shipton-under-Wychwood*, 46–7.

5   *Tales and Legends*, pages 69–84.

ST KENELM : *The Saints in Folklore*, C. Hole, 88–95.

ST AUGUSTINE IN LONG COMPTON : Field, J. E., *The Myth of the Pent Cuckoo*, 152–3.

TOR-BARROW HILL : Rudder, *New History of Gloucestershire*, 347.

FAIR ROSAMUND : This ballad is to be found in I, 347, *seq.* of the Bohn Library edition of *Percy's Reliques*. It has a copious introduction. Stow's account is on 226-7 of the 1695 edition of his *Annales*.

A SERMON UPON MALT : There are several versions of this sermon but they vary very little. The one given is to be found in Part B, II of *A Dictionary of British Folk-Tales in the English Language*, 125–6 and is taken from the British Museum Ms Sloane 3769 ff 21b–22b.

THE MAN WHO ANSWERED THE OWL : This version is to be found in *Through the Lych Gate* by Edward Rainsberry, 125.

MUCKING THE CHURCH TOWER : *loc. cit.*

THE PAINSWICK ANCIENTS : *A Dictionary of British Folk-Tales*, Part A, II, 215 from the Norton Collection.

6   *The Traditions of Wychwood Forest*, pages 85–101.

Good information about the Cornbury estate and the Forest of Wychwood are to be found in V. J. Watney's *Cornbury and the Forest of Wychwood*. This book deals with the varying extent and management of the forest from the late Saxon days onwards.

The de Langleys or Rasors were Chief Foresters of Wychwood from the twelfth century to the middle of the fourteenth.

Arthur Young's account of the state of Wychwood was published in his *General View of the Agriculture of Oxfordshire* in 1809. It is quoted in 205–6 ' Of Cornbury and the Forest of Wychwood '.

HABBERGALLOWS HILL : The chains and irons are now gone but the initials still remain carved on the tree.

Mr Andrews recorded this memorat at his house at Swinbrook in 1971.

This story and the two that follow are to be found in John Kibble's *Historical and Other Notes on Charlbury*, 66–8.

This tale of an even more brutal murder is on 113–17 of *Cider with Rosie*.

M

These tales are to be found in 'Wychwood Forest and Poachers recounted by S. E. Groves, 41–2 and 'Wychwood Forest', 45–6 in *The History of Shipton-under-Wychwood.*

The account of the old woman who had given evidence against James and Pittaway is on 66 of of Kibble's book on Charlbury.

The tale of the lost coffin was told by Dr Thomas Brookes Vicar of Shipton in 1773 and goes back to the reign of Queen Anne: *History of Shipton-under-Wychwood*, 16. The funeral came from Ramsden and the corpse was of a man called Eldridge who was proverbial as a liar.

A short account of the end of the forest fair is given in *Cornbury and the Forest of Wychwood*, 208. This is part of an account of the closing of the forest, 204–8.

7 *Rogues and Highwaymen*, pages 102–108.

Nearly every book which deals with the Burford and Swinbrook area of the Cotswolds gives some account of the Swinbrook Highwaymen. The memorats and local traditions fill out the picture.

The skinning alive of the Bruern shepherd is an oral tradition collected by Mrs Sharp of Asthall Leigh.

The full documentation of the mysterious disappearance of Mr Harrison given in *The Campden Wonder* makes fuller annotation unnecessary.

THE HANGMAN'S STONE: Hartland's *Gloucestershire Folklore*, 51, quoting Rudder, 606. There is another Hangman's Stone with the same story attached to it near Northleach, noted in W. J. Monk's *By Road from Cheltenham to Oxford*, 13.

THE LOCK-UP: This is an oral tradition preserved and transmitted by Mr George Swinford.

8 *Birth, Death and Marriage*, pages 109–117.

CHRISTENING CUSTOMS: 11 of the *Annual Record of the Oxford and District Folklore Society*, 1950.

THE FIRST JOURNEY UPWARDS: Angelina Parker, 'Oxfordshire Village Folklore', *Folklore*, XXXIV, 1923, 326.

TELLING THE BEES: *A.R. of O. & D.F.S.*, 1950, 'Some Oxfordshire Beliefs and Customs Connected with Death and Burial', 11.

WATCHING BY THE DEAD, etc.: *ut supra* 12.

DIVINATION AND MARRIAGE: Most of the charms and beliefs mentioned here are to be found in *A.R. of O. & D.F.S.*, 1952, 6–9. See Appendix for Hemp-seed spell.

THE WIFE-BEATER : *Glos. Notes and Queries*, III, 1887, 70.
ROUGH MUSIC : These examples come from *A.R. of O. & D.F.S.*, 1951, 13–14.

9 *Plants, Trees and Animals*, pages 118–129.

Some useful pieces of plant and flower lore are to be found in the *A.R. of O. & D.F.S.*, 1951, ' Fragments of Oxfordshire Plant-Lore ', 11–13.

ELDER : Another example of the sinister nature of the elder is given by Angelina Parker in *Folklore*, XXXIV (1923), 326. It is in her article ' Oxfordshire Village Folklore II ' and was published after her death : ' It was unlucky to stand under an elder tree when the sun was setting, because the elder tree was supposed to be the tree upon which Judas hanged himself. The person who did so was bewitched.'

UNDER THE ROSE : See the article on the Rose, Radford and Hole, *Encyclopaedia of Superstitions*, 284–6.

THE SLAUGHTERED OAK : Aubrey, *Natural History of Wiltshire*, 53.

SOWING BEANS : *A.R. of O. & D.F.S.*, No. 11 (1959).

THE DEVIL OF WOODSTOCK : Robert Plot, *The Natural History of Oxfordshire*, 210–14.

There are more plant traditions and cures given in the *A.R. of O. & D.F.S.* for 1951 in ' Fragments of Oxfordshire Plant-Lore ', 11–13. Some more planting lore and some scattered pieces of animal lore occur in the no. 11 edition, 1959, unfortunately the last to be published.

KIRTLINGTON LAMB-ALE : *A.R. of O. & D.F.S.*, 1951, 8–9.

THE SPAYED BITCH : R. Plot, *Natural History of Oxfordshire*, 211.

THE FOX WITCH : P. Manning, ' Stray Notes on Oxfordshire Folklore ', *Folklore*, XIII (1902), 289.

RATS AND MICE : *The Encyclopaedia of Superstitions*, 279–80 and 230–1.

BUTTERFLIES : *Encyclopaedia of Superstitions*, 77.

ROBINS : *ut supra* 284 for Oxfordshire items.

ROOKS : *ut supra* 284.

10 *Witches in the Cotswolds*, pages 130–139.

THE LONG COMPTON WITCHES : E. Rainsberry, *Through the Lych Gate*, 126–7. See the Appendix for a record by Percy Manning of an attempt in the same area to nullify a witch's spells by drawing her blood. In this case the necessity of drawing it ' above the breath ' was disregarded, for the witch was wounded in the arm.

Witchcraft element in the Campden Wonder : *The Campden Wonder*, 97.

THE WITCHCRAFT BALLAD : *The Campden Wonder*, 100-seq. The Campden Wonder and Anthony Wood : *The Campden Wonder*, 32.
WITCH-HARE : *Through the Lych Gate*, 128.
SHAKING CHARLOTTE : Angelina Parker, 'Oxfordshire Village Folklore', *Folklore* XXIV, 1913.
THE LITTLE TEW GHOST : A similar poltergeist haunting, also at Little Tew, is recorded by Percy Manning in 'Stray Notes on Oxfordshire Folklore', *Folklore* XIV, 71–2. The victims here were the Halls – a blacksmith's family. They were haunted at Little Tew and the haunting followed them to Hook Norton and Enstone. When they died the haunting ceased. It is unusual for a blacksmith to be the victim of witchcraft because of the power of iron and ironwork.

11 *Supernatural Beliefs*, pages 140–152.

THE WITCH'S GHOST : Kenneth Hare, *Gloucestershire* 89–90.
JACK ADAMS' DEVIL : Angelina Parker, *Folklore* XXXII, 1923, 323.
THE DEVIL IN OXFORDSHIRE : *A.R. of O. & D.F.S.*, 10–12. Angelina Parker also mentions the Devil as a hazard on nutting expeditions.
THE DEVIL : This was in *Folklore*, XXIV, 1913, 84.
THE DEVIL AS BUILDER : Beesley, *The History of Banbury*, 10 (footnote 22).
THE TANFIELDS AT WILCOTE : Sir Laurence Tanfield had once owned and occupied Hill Farm. He had a strange talent for unpopularity. Details of Sir Laurence Tanfield's career are to be found in *Burford Past and Present*, Mrs Sturge Gretton, 78–80.
DAVID TAYLOR'S STORY : *The History of Shipton-under-Wychwood*, 61.
WILCOTE HAUNTINGS : 'Oxfordshire Village Folklore II', *Folklore*, XXXIV, 1923, 323.
SIR JOHN READE : *The History of Shipton-under-Wychwood*, 49.
THE HAUNTING AT BURFORD VICARAGE : See Appendix for the details of this story from W. J. Monk's *By Road from Cheltenham to Oxford*.
THE PEACOCK FARM : Monk, *Drives Round Burford*, 51.
BLACK-STOCKING : Angelina Parker, 'Northleigh Folklore', *Folklore*, XXXII, 1923, 160. According to some accounts only two black legs are to be seen.
THE EDGEHILL GHOSTS : Nugent, *Memorials of John Hampden*, II, 466. (Appendix e.)

12 *Folk Motifs in Cotswold Churches*, pages 153–162.

The Legend of St Christopher is well retold by Christina Hole in *Saints in Folklore*, 51–8, also in Baring-Gould's *Lives of the Saints*.

Ruth Tongue has a fine rustic version of ' St Aloys and the Lame Nag ' in *The Folktales of England*, Briggs and Tongue, 79.

WILCOTE CHURCH: Angelina Parker, ' Oxfordshire Village Folklore ', *Folklore*, XXXII, 1923.

BISLEY CHURCH MOVED BY THE DEVIL: Hartland's *Folklore of Gloucestershire*, 14–15, quoting from *Gloucestershire Notes and Queries*, I, 1881, 390–1.

13 *Trades and Crafts in the Cotswold*, pages 163–171.

' Factors in the Development of the Cotswold Wool Industry ' by R. P. Beckinsale is almost as useful for a knowledge of the wool trade as Arkell's *Oxford Stone* is for the stone quarrying.

A LEGEND OF THE WOOL-MERCHANTS: Evans, *Highways and Byways of Oxfordshire and the Cotswolds* 184–5.

The information about the thirteenth- and fourteenth-century wool trade is from Beckinsale's paper on the Cotswold wool industry, 357–61.

WITNEY BLANKETS: Robert Plot, *Natural History of Oxfordshire*, 283–5.

THE SHUTFORD PLUSH INDUSTRY: Christine Sibbit, *Bells, Blankets, Baskets and Boats*, 36; *Companion into Oxfordshire* 20–2.

THE WOODSTOCK STEEL: Sibbit, 15–16.

WINCHCOMBE TOBACCO: Edith Brill, *The Cotswolds*, 78–9.

BANBURY CHEESE: A brief note of Christine Sibbit's, 4–5, mentions this cheese recipe which I quote from Percy Manning's Ms collection to be found in the Bodleian Library.

Appendices

The Randwick Wap Modernised

WHAT IS THE WAP?

RANDWICK WAP has been held in the hillside village of Ranwick, two miles north-west of Stroud in the Cotswolds, for hundreds and hundreds of years as a Spring Festival. There was a break in the tradition of about sixty years or so until 1972, but this break is comparatively small compared with the length of time that the Wap has taken place in the village.

We are indebted to Miss E. Fennemore's 'History of Randwick' published in 1893 for preserving the important details of the Wap ceremonies, and as many of these as possible have been faithfully maintained for your interest and entertainment.

Prior to the Wap (at the beginning of April) a Mayor of Randwick has been 'chas'd in' (which means elected) from among the residents of the Parish. One of the central features of the Wap is the enthronement of this Mayor at the Mayor's Pool. This is by the main road through the village, a little way below the Parish Church. The Mayor is carried down to the Pool from the War Memorial near where the village Stocks used to be. He sits in the special 'Mayor's Chair' and is borne by four Stalwarts. The Mopman leads the procession, and clears the way for it with his wet mop. Then come four boys carrying whitened rods tied with knots of ribbon. Then follows the Mayor. His sceptre is a wooden bowl from which he sprinkles water on the spectators. On his right walks the High Sheriff, and on his left the Sword Bearer. Then comes a small band of musicians. At the back of the procession is a Flagman.

When the Mayor's Procession has reached the Pool the Mayor's Chair is set down in the water for the singing of the Mayor's Song, which is printed on the back of this programme. All are invited to join in as much as they can.

Now there is another very ancient Spring ceremony, peculiar to the village of Randwick as far as is known. This is the CHEESE-ROLLING. This used to take place from very ancient times on May Day – now the first Saturday in May to be more convenient. Three Double Gloucester cheeses are taken in procession being either carried or wheeled on litters. They are adorned with Spring flowers. When they reach the Parish Church there is a short Service in the Churchyard, and then they are taken off their litters and prepared for the Rolling. Each cheese is rolled three times mystically around the Church building before being rolled down a steep slope after which they are cut up into pieces for general consumption.

The very ancient Cheese Procession has a modern flavour in that it has become a proper carnival led by a Band – this year the Avening Silver Band – and has the Ladies of the Wap to match the Lords who come down to meet them at the Mayor's Pool. The Ladies of the Wap include the Wap Queen and her two Ladies in Waiting on a horse-drawn conveyance. In front of these go the six May Princesses (ages 5 to 11). In addition, anyone is invited to join the Cheese Procession in fancy dress. This procession starts from Cashes Green Hospital and comes directly up the road to meet the Mayor's Procession at the Pool at 2.15 p.m.

After the Mayor's Song the Mayor goes up with the Wap Queen to the Church for the Cheese Rolling in which both have an active part. When the Churchyard Service is over and the Cheese Rolling begins the six bells of the Parish Church are rung to signify the official opening of the Stalls.

Besides the Stalls there are a good number and variety of traditional country entertainments with plenty of Morris Dancers, Mummers, Country Dancers and Singers to be seen and heard – in fact it is the hope of us all that once you have seen how the Randwick Wap is a unique blend of ancient and modern you will want to become a regular visitor on the first Saturday in May.

RANDWICK WAP
Saturday 5 May 1973
Programme of Events
(All Times p.m.)

1.00 Informal Tour of Cashes Green Hospital Wards by the Wap Queen, Ladies-in-Waiting and Cheesebearers.

1.15 Judging begins for the FREE FANCY DRESS COMPETITION for all those of any age who wish to take part in the Cheese Procession from Cashes Green Hospital to the Mayor's Pool.

1.30 Recommended latest time of arrival at Cashes Green Hospital of those who wish to take part in the Cheese Procession.

1.50 Procession leaves Cashes Green Hospital and proceeds direct to Randwick.

2.00 Enthronement of the Mayor at the War Memorial.

2.05   Mayor's Procession leaves for the Pool.
2.15   Mayor's Song at the Pool.
2.30   Open Air Service in the Churchyard.
2.45   Cheese Rolling begins.
       Stalls Open
       Other Entertainments (see page 5) take place at various times and locations during the afternoon, in the area between the Parish Church and the Village Hall.
5.30   Market Closes.
6.00   The Vine Tree Inn and Carpenters Arms open and welcome visitors.
8.00   GRAND CEILIDH AT THE VILLAGE HALL
       Country Dancing till Midnight with GERRY PHELPS and the KAYLEA BIRDS. Admission 25p at the Door. LICENSED BAR

SUPPLEMENTARY ENTERTAINMENTS
AFTERNOON
MORRIS DANCING by the GLOUCESTERSHIRE MORRIS MEN and OLD SPOT MORRIS MEN
COUNTRY DANCING by the CHELTENHAM SQUARE CLUB
SINGING by the WESTANDERS
PUNCH AND JUDY by D. Strange
MAYPOLE DANCING by the Randwick Brownies
CUP FINAL IN COLOUR by DANIELS of Kings Stanley (Village Hall)
TOWN CRIER Mr Keith Glover
ART EXHIBITION at the School Terrapin Classroom, of works by members of the LILLIAN LINSELL ART GROUP and MR PATRICK FARRELL and other local Artists. Some works will be for sale. Children's work will also be on show in other school classrooms (admission free).
FLORAL DISPLAY at the Parish Church, with exhibition of some items of local historical interest (admission free).
MUMMER'S PLAYS by the CITY OF GLOUCESTER MUMMERS and the WINCHCOMBE PLAY by EXMOUTH ARMS FOLK CLUB GROUP from Cheltenham.
A FILM OF THE RANDWICK WAP 1972 will be shown at intervals in the afternoon at RANDWICK METHODIST CHAPEL by Mr Clifford Smith of the Cotswold Cine Club: he also made the film (sound and colour) himself.
IN THE EVENING from 8 p.m. until midnight the GRAND CEILIDH will take place at the Village Hall. Caller for Country Dancing: GERRY PHELPS. The KAYLEA BIRDS BAND and the EXMOUTH ARMS FOLK SONG CLUB SINGERS will provide the Music. ALL WELCOME. Admission at Door 25p. LICENSED BAR.

THE WAP FREEMEN

If you have reached the age of 18 years you are cordially invited to become a RANDWICK WAP FREEMAN.

This will give you two important privileges connected with this unique Festival :

FIRST You will be entitled to chuse in (that means 'vote for') next year's and future years' 'Mayor of Randwick'. Only the Wap Freemen are entitled to vote for the Mayor.

SECOND You will receive through the post advance information of next year's Wap, which, as always, will be on the first Saturday in May.

Together with your advance information you will also receive your voting form for next year's Chusing In of the Mayor. These will be sent to you about the middle of March.

HOW TO BECOME A WAP FREEMAN

You can only become a Wap Freeman by signing your name in the POLE BOOK. On Wap Day this can be found at the Wap Committee's Stall. There is a small registration fee of 10p.

The Wap Committee hope that you will take this opportunity to join the many friends & supporters of this very ancient and traditional festival, which is unique to the village of Randwick.

LORDS OF THE WAP 1973

MAYOR OF RANDWICK   Mr David P. Harmer

HIGH SHERIFF   Mr Royston Dean

SWORD BEARER   Mr Maurice H. J. Baker

MOPMAN   Mr Royston V. Davis

LADIES OF THE WAP 1973

WAP QUEEN   Miss Mary Morrison

LADIES IN WAITING   Miss Susan Watkins and Miss Carol McMurtrie

It is interesting to see the hand of modernism laid on these traditional festivities. A care for the tradition is evident in this celebration and it is inevitable that it should be prettified and sophisticated if it is to be preserved. The attempt to keep it up at all is laudable. The pamphlet is of course peppered with advertisements, among them one notes :

Why not

MAKE A DAY OF IT

visiting STROUD in the morning

and having a good, satisfying, old-fashioned

FISH & CHIP LUNCH

Appendix to Chapter 3

BURFORD MUMMER'S PLAY

Characters

Turkish Knight
Father Christmas
King of Egypt
St George
Dragon
Giant
Doctor

ENTER TURKISH KNIGHT WITH A RUSH :

Open your doors, and let us in,
For I hope your favours we will win,
Whether I rise or whether I fall,
We will do our best to please you all.
St George is here, and swears he will come in :
If he does he will pierce my skin.
If you do not believe what I do say
Ask Father Christmas to come in and clear the way.

FATHER CHRISTMAS :

In comes old Father Christmas, welcome or welcome not,
For I hope old Father Christmas will never be forgot.
I am not come here to laugh or to jeer
But for a pocketful of money and a skinful of beer.
If you do not believe what I do say
I will ask the King of Egypt to come in, so clear the way.

KING OF EGYPT :

Here am I, the King of Egypt,
So boldly do appear,
St George, St George, walk in,
My only son and heir.
Walk in, my son St George,
And boldly act thy part,
So that all the people here
May see thy wondrous heart.

ST GEORGE :

Here am I, St George,
From Britain did I spring,
And I will fight the fiery Dragon
My wonders to begin.
I'll clip his wings,
He shall not fly.

I'll cut him down
Or else I die.

DRAGON APPEARS :

Who is he that seeks the dragon's blood?
And speaks so angry and so loud?
That English dog, will he before me stand,
I'll cut him down with my courageous hand.
With my long teeth and scurvy jaws
Of such I break up half a score,
Then stay my stomach till I have more.

ST GEORGE AND DRAGON FIGHT. ST GEORGE IS OVERCOME, AND FATHER
CHRISTMAS CALLS :

Is there a Doctor to be found, all ready near at hand,
To cure a deep and deadly wound, and make a champion stand?

DOCTOR :

Oh yes, there is a Doctor to be found, already near at hand,
To cure a deep and deadly wound, and make a champion stand.

FATHER CHRISTMAS :

And what do you cure?

DOCTOR :

All sorts of diseases, whatever you pleases,
The physic, the palsy and the gout,
If the Devil's in I'll blow him out.

FATHER CHRISTMAS :

What is your fee?

DOCTOR :

£15 is my fee, the money to lay down,
But as to such a rogue as thee, I'll cure thee for £10.

TAKES A PILL FROM THE BAG, AND BOTTLE, AND GOES TO ST
GEORGE.

DOCTOR :

I carry a little bottle of Alexopain :
Here, Jack, take a little of my flip-flop,
Pour it down thy tip-top,
Rise up and fight again.

ST GEORGE AND DRAGON FIGHT AGAIN, AND THE DRAGON DIES.

ST GEORGE :

Here am I, St George, that worthy champion bold,
And with my sword and spear I won three crowns of gold.
I fought the fiery dragon, and brought him to the slaughter,
And by that I won fair Sabra, the King of Egypt's daughter.
Now where is that man who will me defy?
I'll cut his giblets full of holes,
And make his buttons fly.

TURKISH KNIGHT ENTERS :
> Here come I, the Turkish Knight,
> And have come from the Turkish land to fight :
> I'll fight St George, who is my foe,
> And I'll make him yield before I go.
> He brags to such a high degree,
> And thinks that none can do the likes of he.

ST GEORGE :
> Where is the Turk that will before me stand?
> I'll cut him down with my courageous hand.

ST GEORGE STRIKES TURKISH KNIGHT, WHO KNEELS BEFORE HIM.

TURKISH KNIGHT :
> Oh pardon me, St George, pardon of thee I crave,
> Oh pardon me this night, and I will be thy slave.

ST GEORGE :
> No pardon will you have, while I have foot to stand,
> O rise thee up again, and strike out, sword in hand.

ST GEORGE AND TURKISH KNIGHT FIGHT, AND TURKISH KNIGHT IS
VANQUISHED.

GIANT ENTERS :
> In come I, the Giant,
> Bold Turpin is my name,
> And all the nations round
> Do tremble at my fame.
> Where'er I go they tremble at my sight,
> No lord or champion long with me will fight.

ST GEORGE :
> Here is one that dares to look thee in the face :
> I'll soon send thee to another place.

GIANT WOUNDED.

FATHER CHRISTMAS :
> Is there a Doctor to be found already near at hand.
> To cure a deep and deadly wound, and make a champion stand?

DOCTOR :
> Yes, there is a Doctor to be found, already near at hand,
> To cure a deep and deadly wound, and make a champion stand.

FATHER CHRISTMAS :
> What can you cure?

DOCTOR :
> All sorts of diseases, whatever you pleases,
> The physic, the palsy and the gout,
> If the Devil's in I'll blow him out.

FATHER CHRISTMAS :
> And what is your fee?

DOCTOR :
   £15 is my fee, the money to lay down,
   But as for such a rogue as thee, I'll cure thee for £10.
DOCTOR PRODUCES MEDICINE AGAIN.
DOCTOR :
   I carry a little bottle of Alexopain,
   Here, Jack, take a little of this flip-flop
   And pour it down thy tip-top.
   Rise up and do not fight again,
   Do not fight again.
FATHER CHRISTMAS :
   Now ladies and gentlemen, your sport is most ended,
   So prepare for the box, which is highly commended.
   The box which would speak, if it had but a tongue,
   Come throw in your money, and think it's no wrong.

Appendix to Chapter 8

Hempseed at Christmas

(from *Folklore*, XCIV, 1923, Angelina Parker, ' Oxfordshire Village
Folklore' II, 324)

There were at Northleigh, as at Handborough, many charms
practised by girls in hopes of seeing their future husbands. Mrs
Calcutt's mother was probably the last girl to try the charm of
sowing hempseed to make hers appear. She, with a girl friend, went
to the churchyard one Christmas Eve at midnight, carrying some
hempseed, and while throwing it over her left shoulder said :

     I sow hempseed,
     Hempseed I sow,
     He that is to be my husband,
     Come after me and mow,
     Not in his best or Sunday array,
     But in his clothes he wears every day!

The friend with her was very much frightened : some people said
she saw a coffin, but whatever she saw, or thought she saw, it is
certain she died soon afterwards, and the people in the village
evidently connected her death in some way with the visit to the
churchyard, and they forbade their daughters to try this charm
any more.

Appendix to Chapter 10

(from Manning's 'Stray Notes on Oxfordshire Folklore', *Folklore* XIII, 290)

Some forty years ago there lived at Salford, near Chipping Norton, an old woman named Dolly Henderson, a notable witch. One day she fell out with a woman named Ann Hulver, and bewitched her, so that she was very ill for a long time and could get no cure. At last she went to a cunning man named Manning, who told her that she would meet a woman as she went home, and that she was the person who had caused her illness, but she was not to speak to her, or say anything to anyone about her. But she did; she told some women that worked in the fields what the man said, and so she got worse and worse till she was like a skeleton. About this time a boy was also bewitched by old Dolly, and his brother threw a thorn stick at her, which tore her arm and made it bleed a good deal. The woman and the boy then soon got well, but the old witch died, and the terror of the village was got rid of. (From Mrs Jinny Bigerstaff of Salford, aged 63, who knew the people mentioned – 9th October, 1897.)

Appendix to Chapter 11

A Burford Ghost Story

(from *By Road from Cheltenham to Oxford*, by W. J. Monk, 61–2).

The Vicar of Burford, in 1668, was the Rev. John Thorpe, and it would appear that a curate-in-charge of the parish later was a certain Rev. W. G. Underwood. It seems, moreover, that the latter lived at Burford Vicarage. Now, the descendants of this Mr Underwood, in searching through some old documents not long ago, came across a parchment book in which were several entries from the Burford Registers, and included in these papers was a note relating the following circumstances: 'Mrs George Underwood, the wife of the Rev. G. W. Underwood, had just moved into the Vicarage of Burford, Oxon., with her husband, and was arranging an upstairs room, when a ring at the door announced a visitor, who was admitted. The servant came up to tell her mistress she had shown a lady who did not give her name into the drawing room. Mrs Underwood went down, but found no one in the room, but as there were windows opening into a small garden she concluded her visitor had gone there and stepped out in search of her. But there was no one to be seen, and as there was no egress from the garden she was much astonished, and questioned the servant closely as to the appearance of the lady. The maid described the brown dress and appearance of the lady as rather peculiar, the face forbidding. Some other ladies in the parish were calling afterwards, and Mrs Underwood, repeating the description, asked them if they could tell who her mysterious visitor was. They were much astonished, and exclaimed she must have been Mrs Thorpe, who was the wife of the last incumbent, and had died, I think, before him. They also said she had not been liked, and that there were some uncomfortable stories about her and the disappearance of young children who had come to be with her. Some time afterwards an alteration was made in the garden, and in one part bones of young children were found. Nothing more was ever known.'

Select Bibliography

PERIODICALS AND PAMPHLETS CONSULTED

Annual Record of the Oxfordshire and District Folklore Society, Nos. I–XI, 1949–62. (See Notes for particular items)

R. P. BECKINSALE, 'Factors in the Development of the Cotswold Woollen Industry', *Geographical Journal*, IX, 1937

Cambridge Morris Men, 25th Anniversary, 1949

JAMES DYER, *Discovering Regional Archaeology in the Cotswolds and the Upper Thames*, Shire Publications, 1970

A. J. EVANS, 'The Folklore of the Rollright Stones', *The Folklore Journal*, VI, 1895

Gloucestershire Notes and Queries, 1881–90

EVELYN GOSHAWK, *Idbury History*, 1961

'G.T.S.S.' *All Saints, Bisley Church Guide*

JOHN KIBBLE, Manuscript collection of traditional material lodged in Woodstock Museum

E. T. LONG, *The Wall Paintings in Shorthampton Church*

P. MANNING, *Stray Notes on Oxfordshire Folklore, Folklore*, XIV, 1903

R. R. MARETT, 'The Little Tew Ghost', *Folklore*, XLIV, 1933

ANGELINA PARKER, 'Village Folklore', *Folklore*, XXIV, 1913

REV. W. H. SEDDON, *Painswick Feast*, December 1921

CHRISTINE SIBBIT, *Bells, blankets, baskets and boats, a survey of crafts and industries in Oxfordshire*, Oxford City and County Museum, 1968

GEORGE SWINFORD, 'Old Sports of Filkins', *Annual Record of the Oxfordshire and District Folklore Society*, II, 1950

DAVID and DIANNE UTLEY, *Discovering Gloucestershire and the Cotswolds*, Shire Publications, 1969

BOOKS CITED AND CONSULTED

W. J. ARKELL, *Oxford Stone*, republished S. R. Publishers, 1970

SIR ROBERT ATKYNS, *The Ancient and Present State of Golucestershire*, 1712

W. ST CLAIR BADDELEY, *A History of Cirencester*, 1924

S. BARING-GOULD, *Lives of the Saints*, 16 vols, 1914

E. W. BAUGHMAN, *Type and Motif-Index of the Folktales of England and North America*, 1966

ALFRED BEESLEY, *The History of Banbury*, 1841

F. G. BRABANT, *Oxfordshire*, 4th edition (revised), Methuen, 1924

R. BRAITHWAITE, *Drunken Barnaby's Four Journeys* (Elegies and Satires), 1615

N

KATHARINE M. BRIGGS, *A Dictionary of British Folk-Tales*, Routledge, 1970

EDITH BRILL, *The Cotswolds* (County Books series), 1955

Camden's Britannia, Newly Translated into English with large Additions and Improvements by Edmund Gibson, 1695

SIR GEORGE CLARK (ed.), *The Campden Wonder*, 1959

R. G. COLLINGWOOD, *Roman Britain*, 1934

J. CHARLES COX, *Gloucestershire*, 4th edition (revised), 1924

O. G. S. CRAWFORD, *Long Barrows of the Cotswolds*, 1925

P. H. DITCHFIELD, *Memorials of Old Oxfordshire*, 1903

HERBERT A. EVANS, *Highways and Byways in Oxford and the Cotswolds*, 1938

J. MEADE FALKNER, *A History of Oxfordshire* (Popular County Histories series), 1906

J. E. FIELD, *The Myth of the Pent Cuckoo, a study in Folklore*, 1913

GEOFFREY OF MONMOUTH, *British History*, contained in *Six Old English Chronicles*, Bohn's Library, 1848

ALICE GOMME, *Dictionary of Singing Games*, 2 vols, 1898

MARY STURGE GRETTON, *Burford Past and Present*, 3rd edition (revised), 1945

R. H. GRETTON, *The Burford Records*, 1920

MURIEL GROVES, *The History of Shipton-under-Wychwood*, 1934

KENNETH HARE, *Gloucestershire* (County Books series), no date

S. HARTLAND, *County Folklore of Gloucestershire*, 1892

JACQUETTA HAWKES, *A Land*

W. C. HAZLITT, *Fairy Tales, Legends and Romances Illustrating Shakespeare*, 1875

ALEX HELM and N. PEACOCK, *English Ritual Drama*, 1967

CHRISTINA HOLE, *Saints in Folklore*, 1965

Holinshed's Chronicle, 3 vols, 2nd edition, 1587

EDWARD HUTTON, *Highways and Byways in Gloucestershire*, 1936

JOHN KIBBLE, *Historical and other Notes on the Ancient Manor of Charlbury and its nine Hamlets*, 1927

LAURIE LEE, *Cider with Rosie*, 1973

John Leland's Itinerary (edited Hearne), 9 vols, 1710

GERVASE MARKHAM, *The English Husbandman*, 1612

ARTHUR MEE, *Gloucestershire* (King's England series), 1947

W. J. MONK, *History of Burford*, London, 1891

WILLIAM J. MONK, *By Road from Cheltenham to Oxford*, 1922

W. J. MONK, *Walks and Drives Round Burford*, 1896

REGINALD NETTEL, *Sing a Song of England*, 1954

LORD NUGENT, *Memorials of John Hampden*, 2 vols, London, 1832

PETER and IONA OPIE, *Oxford Dictionary of Nursery Rhymes*, 1951

E. H. PARTRIDGE, *Collectanea of Oxford Folklore*, 1912

Percy's Reliques of Ancient English Poetry (J. V. Prichard ed.), Bohn Library, 1900

ROBERT PLOT, *The Natural History of Oxfordshire*, London, 1705

E. and M. A. RADFORD and C. HOLE, *Encyclopaedia of Superstitions*, revised edition, 1962

EDWARD RAINSBERRY, *Through the Lych Gate*, 1969

SAMUEL RUDDER, *New History of Gloucestershire*, 1779

Six Old English Chronicles (J. A. Giles ed.), Bohn Library, 1848

JOIIN STOW, *The Annales of England*, 1695

JAMES TAIT, 'Richard Whittington', *Dictionary of National Biography*

FLORA THOMPSON, *Lark Rise to Candleford*, 1945

R. J. E. TIDDY, *The Mummers' Play*, 1923

RUTH L. TONGUE, 'Somerset Folklore', *County Folklore*, VIII, 1965

H. D. TRAILL, *Social England*, 6 vols, illustrated edition n.d., but circa 1890

PETER UNDERWOOD, *A Gazetteer of British Ghosts*, 1971

E. R. VYVYAN (ed.), *Cotswold Games, Annalia Dubrensia*, 1970

VERNON J. WATNEY, *Cornbury and the Forest of Wychwood*, 1910

William of Malmesbury's English Chronicle, Bohn's Antiquarian Library, 1847

ALFRED WILLIAMS, *Folksongs of the Upper Thames*, 1923

ETHEL CARLETON WILLIAMS, *Companion into Oxfordshire*, 4th edition, 1951

ANTHONY WOOD, *Athenae Oxonienses*, vol 1, 1961; *Fasti*, 1962

A. R. WRIGHT and T. E. LONES, *British Calendar Customs*, 1938

MUSEUMS OF FOLKLORE INTEREST

Asthall : Farm Museum (Christopher Walker)
Bilbury : Mill Museum (not exclusively local)
Burford : Tolsey Museum (mainly historical)
Burford : Filkins Museum (private, by appointment only)
Chastleton House (some objects of folklore interest)
Painswick Museum (small)
Stratford-upon-Avon : Farm Museum at Mary Arden's House
Woodstock : Oxfordshire County Museum (more industrial than folklore)

The Folklore and Folk Life Museum at Reading, though right outside the Cotswold Area, is well worth a visit.

Index of Tale Types

The distinction between tale-types and motifs may not be clear to people who are not specialists in folk-tales. A tale-type is the whole plot of a tale – say, Cinderella – with all its various strands and a motif is the name given to the strands of a tale, as for instance ' cruel stepmother ', ' fairy godmother ', ' magic transformation ' in the Cinderella story. The tale-types were given their present classification by Antti Aarne and Stith Thompson. Not many legends were treated in the tale-type index, however, and they received a partial treatment in Reidar Christiansen's *The Migratory Legends* in 1958.

In this list numbers preceded by AT are from the Aarne-Thompson type index; those with ML are from *The Migratory Legends* of R. Christiansen; those with ML and an asterisk are thus classified in K. M. Briggs's *A Dictionary of British Folk-Tales*. A further index was made of English and North American types and motifs by E. Baughman, and the word ' Baughman ' following a type or motif indicates that this is one of his classifications.

Motif Index

General Index